mode Parisienne

FOR CONSTANCE.

MODE PARISIENNE

CLÉMENT DEZELUS

GINGKO PRESS

C'EST L'AUTOMNE...

PERSONALIZE YOUR BAG WITH AUTUMN COLORS

MAKE-UP WITH YOUR FAVORITE BRUSHES

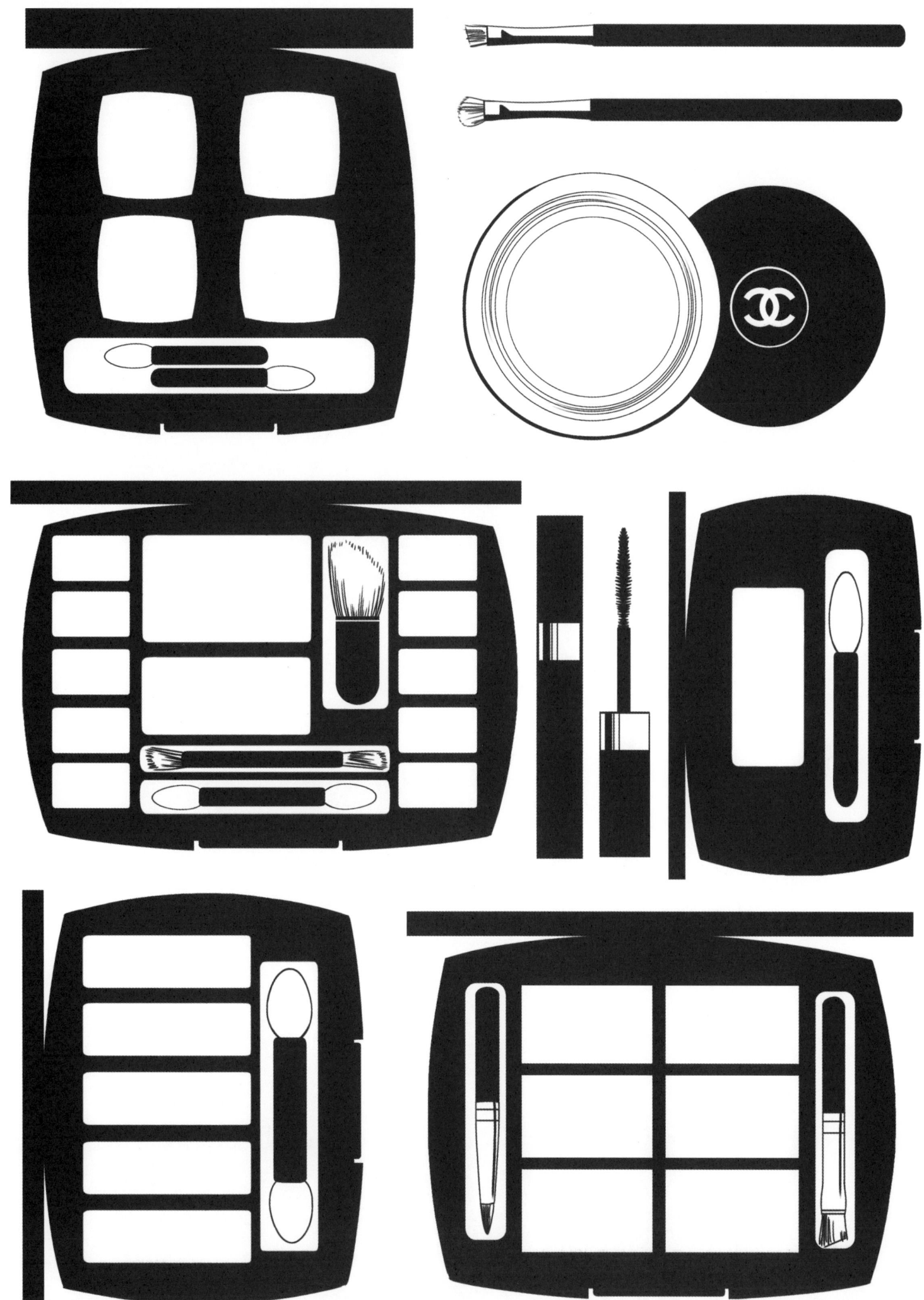

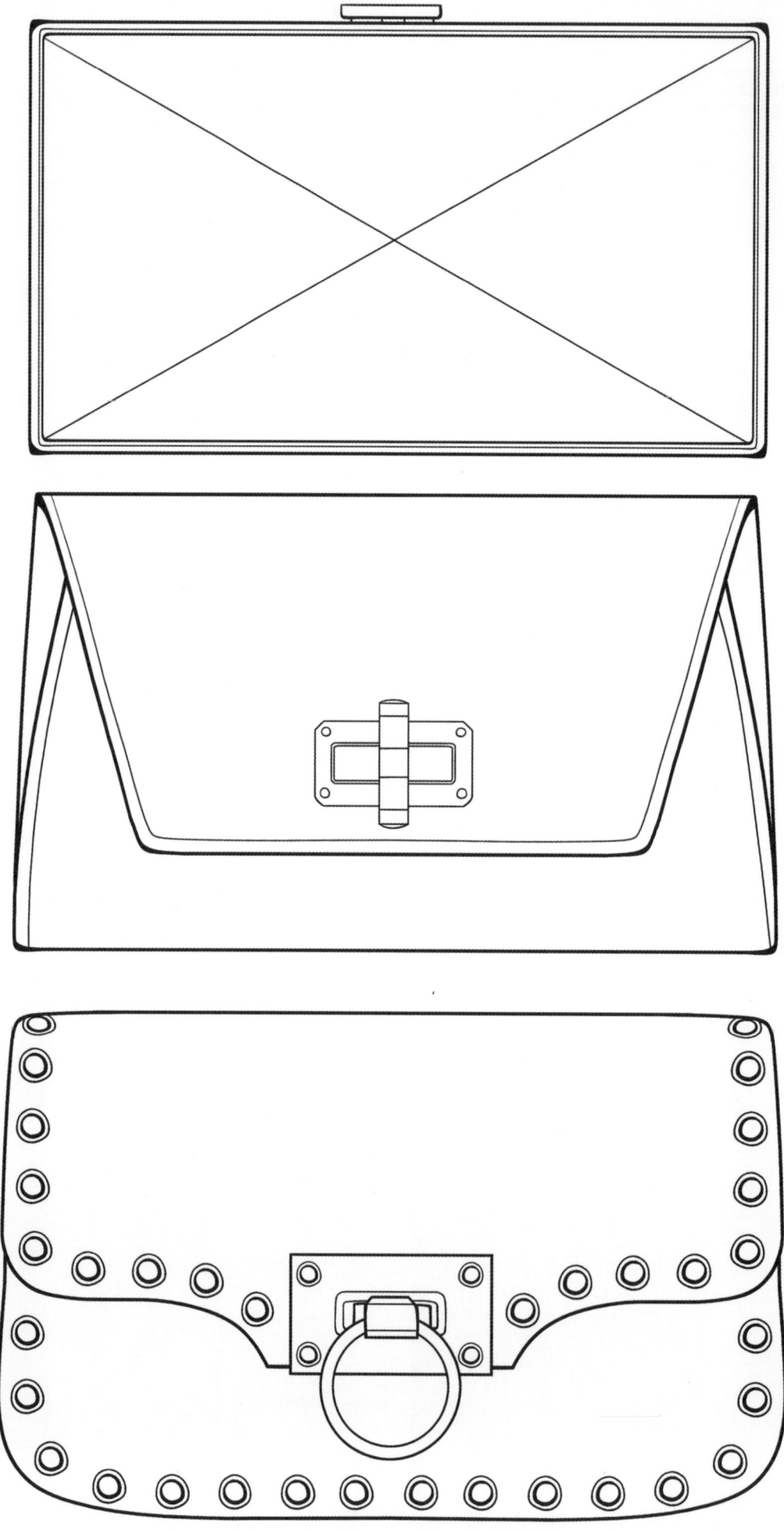

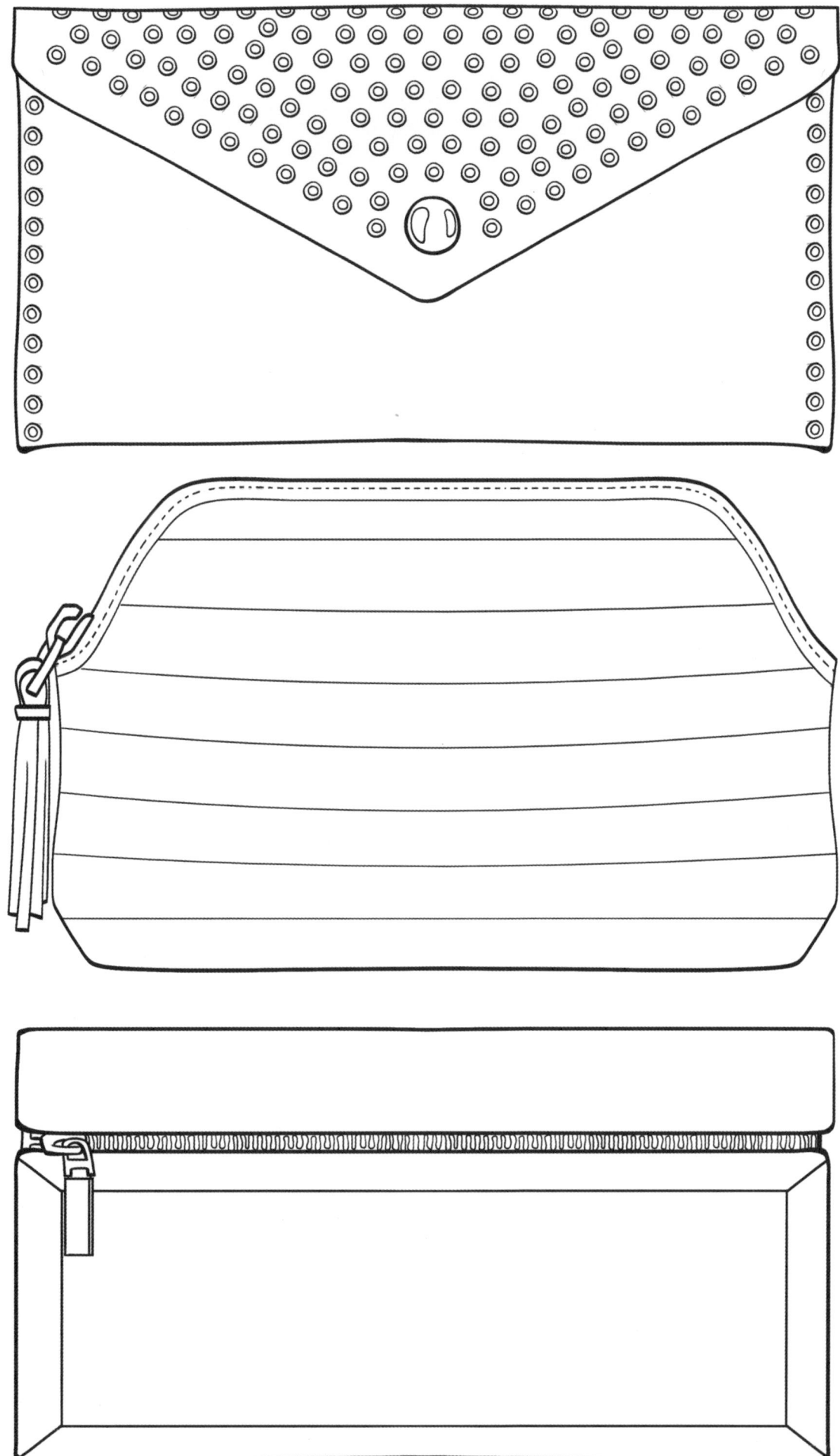

FILL IN THE COLOR OF YOUR FAVORITE LEATHER JACKET

mademoiselle MONTAIGNE

DRESS YOUR NEW PURCHASES IN
COLOR

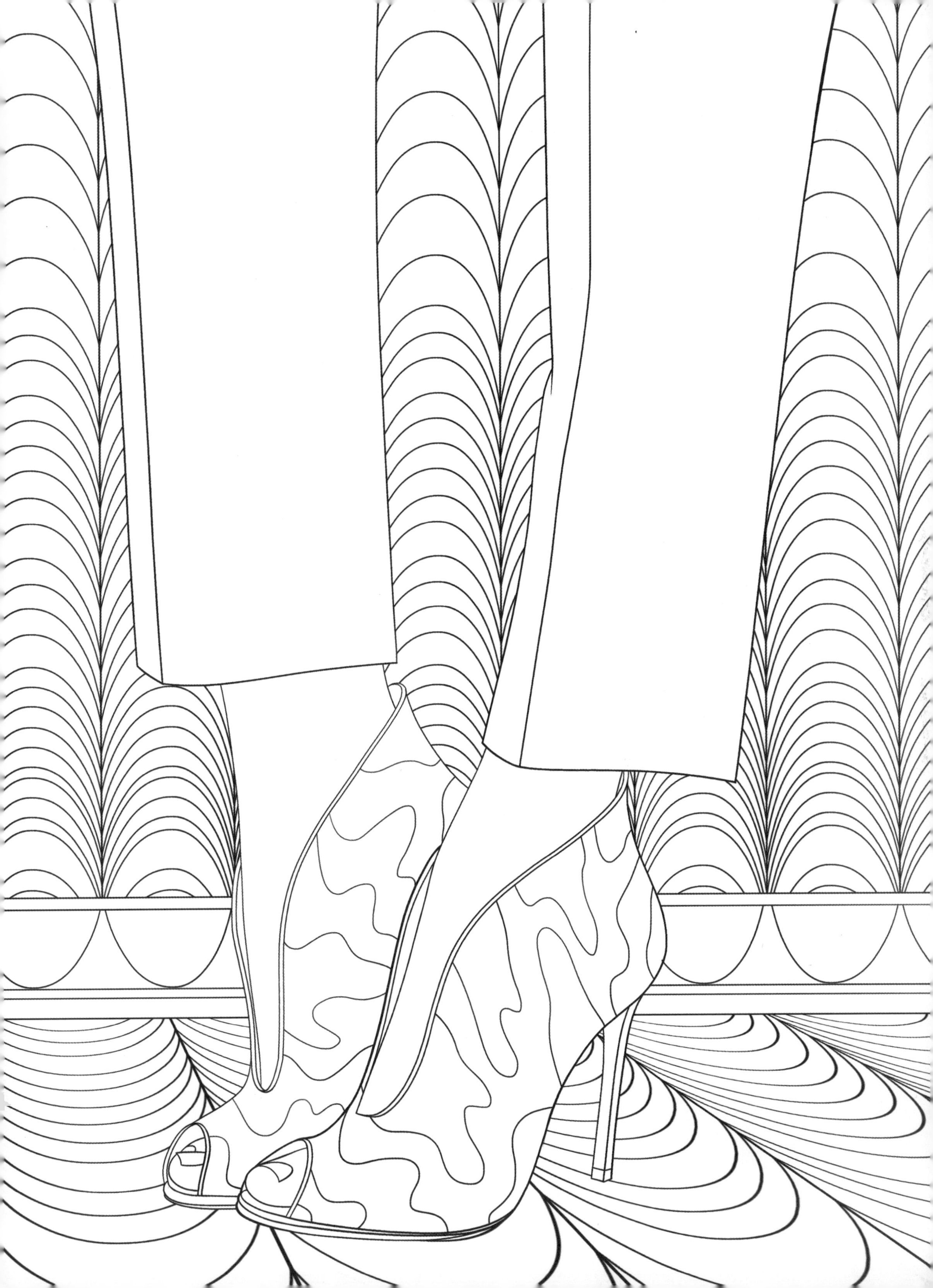

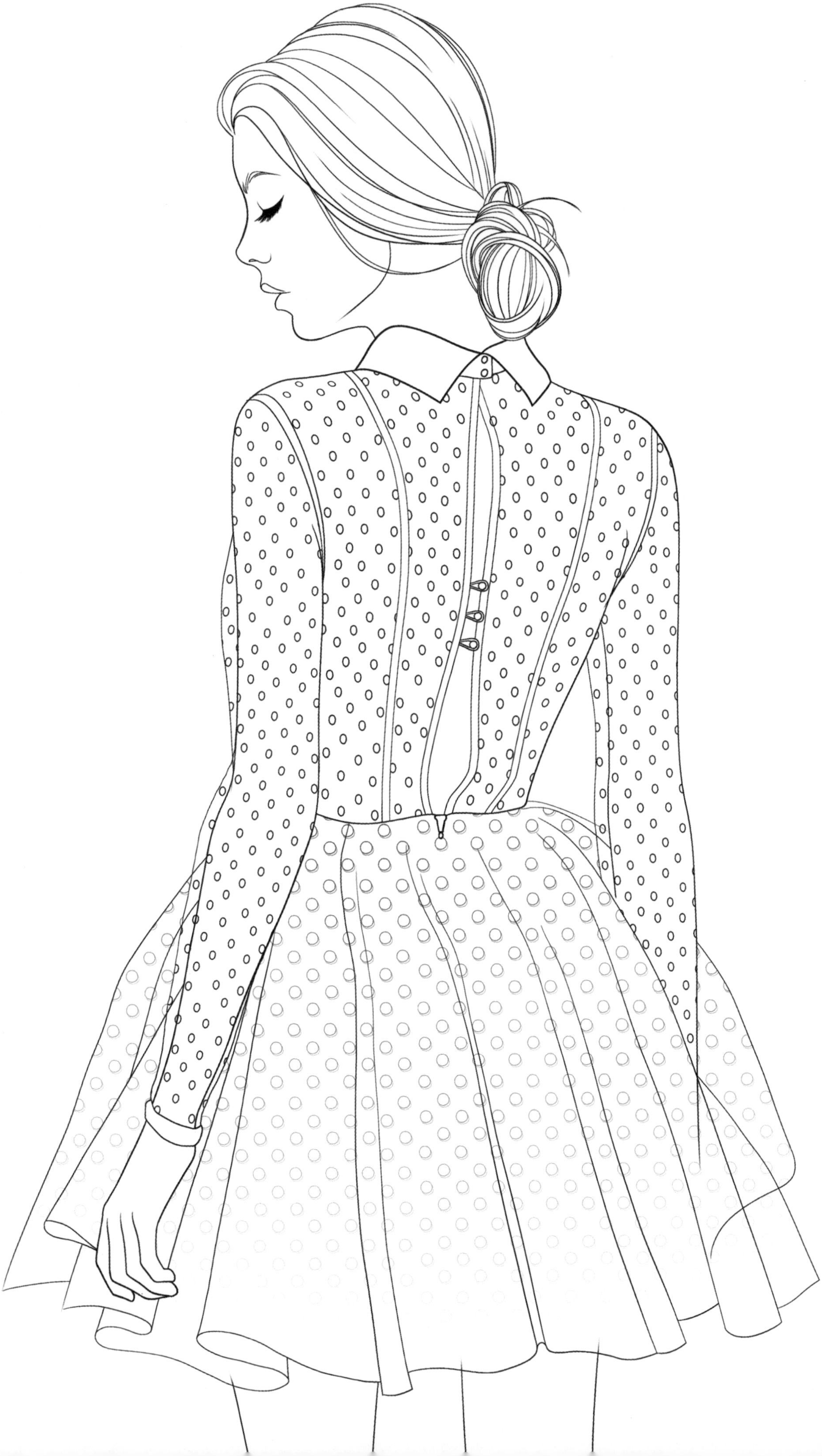

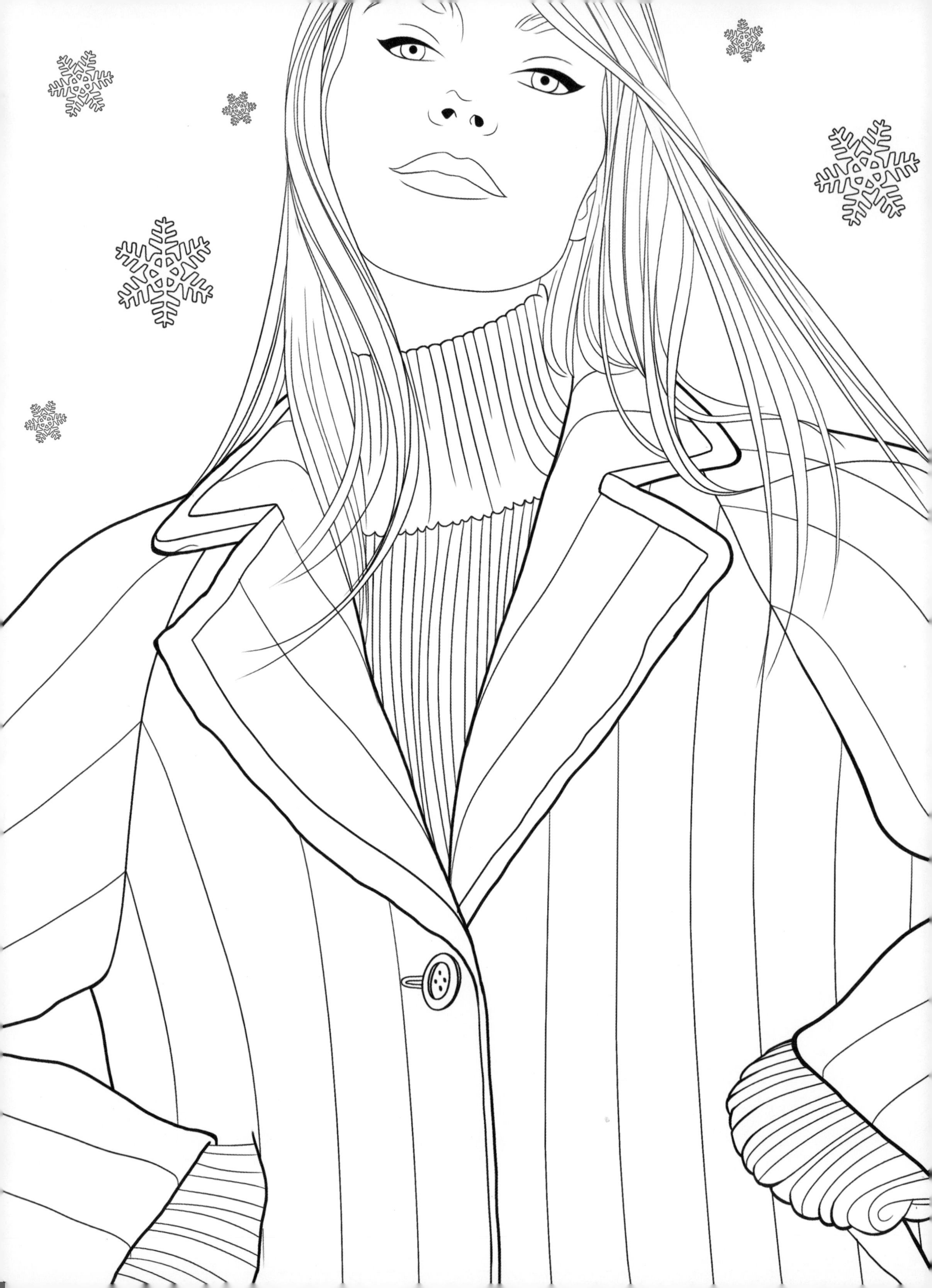

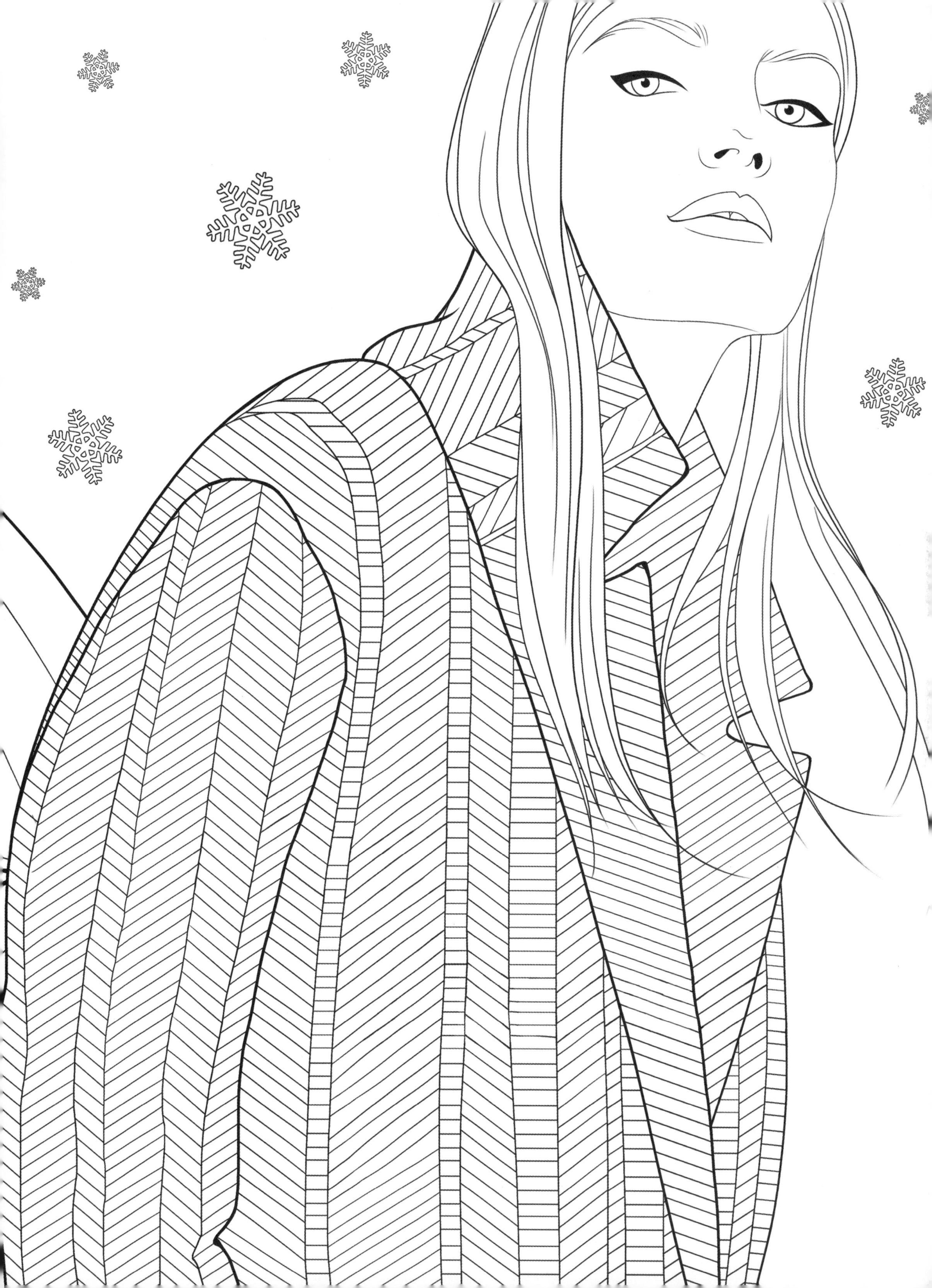

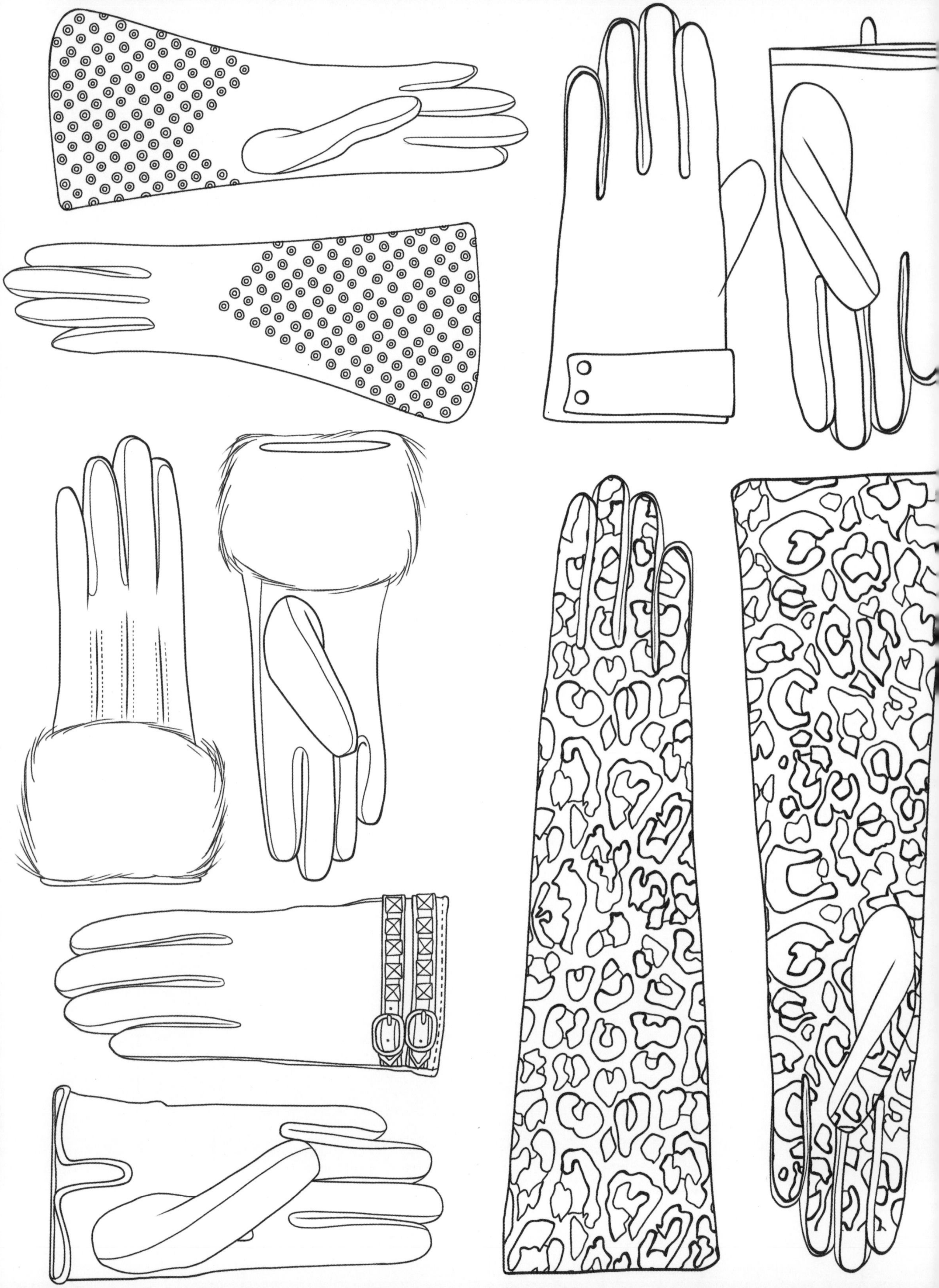

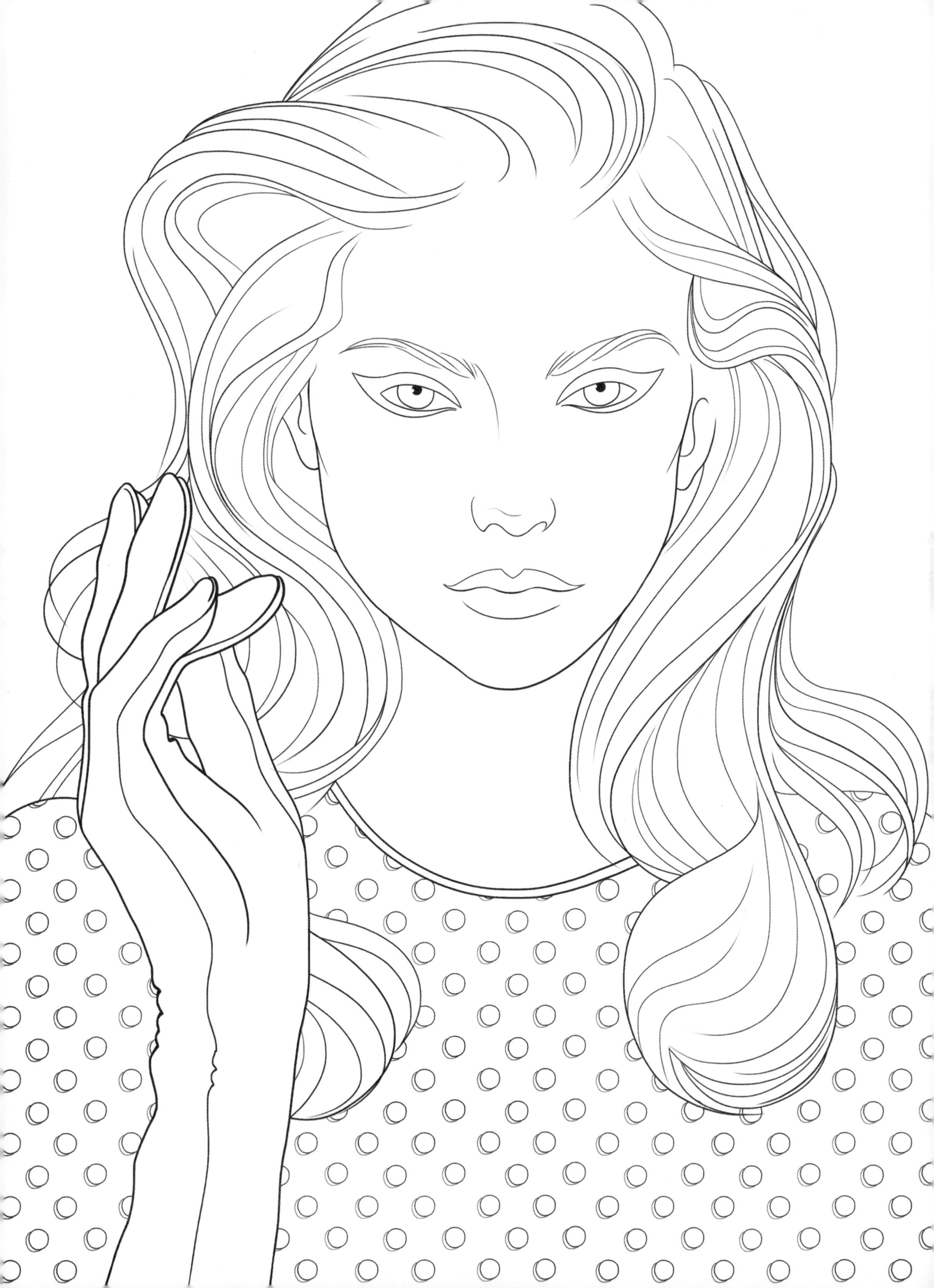

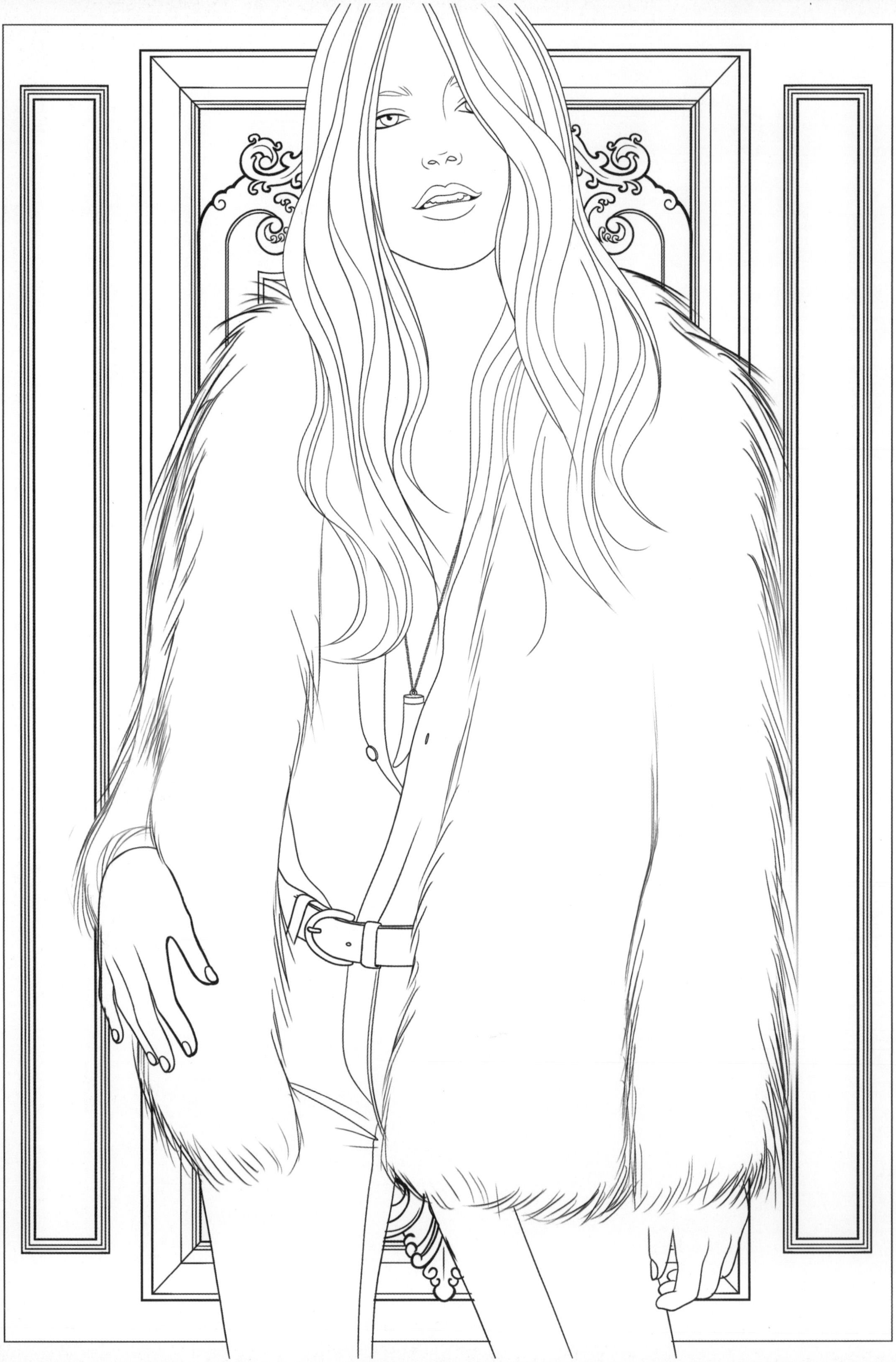

MANTEAU DE FOURRURE

STRIPES

SPOTTED

ONE COLOR

BLACK

MULTI-COLOR

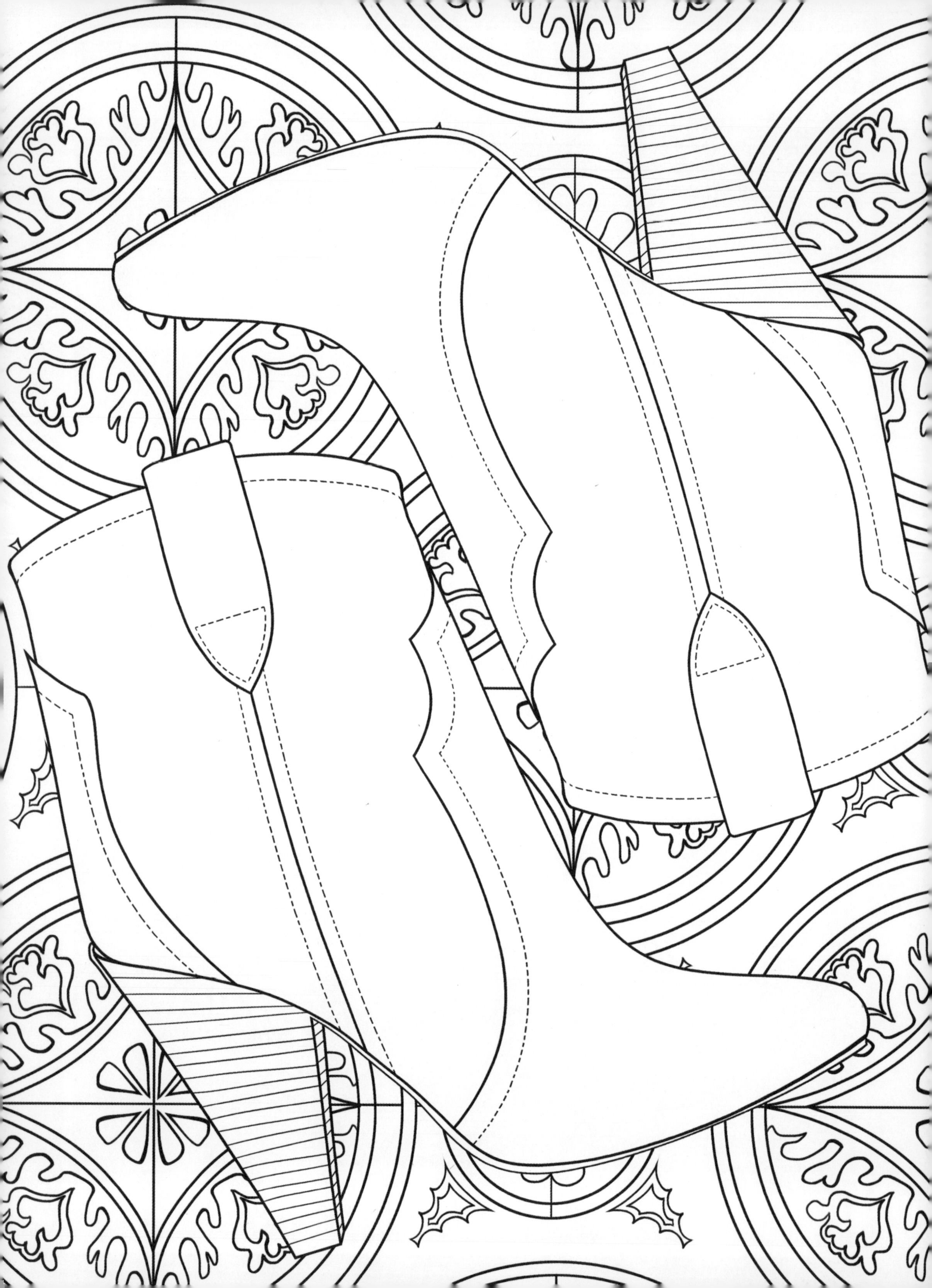

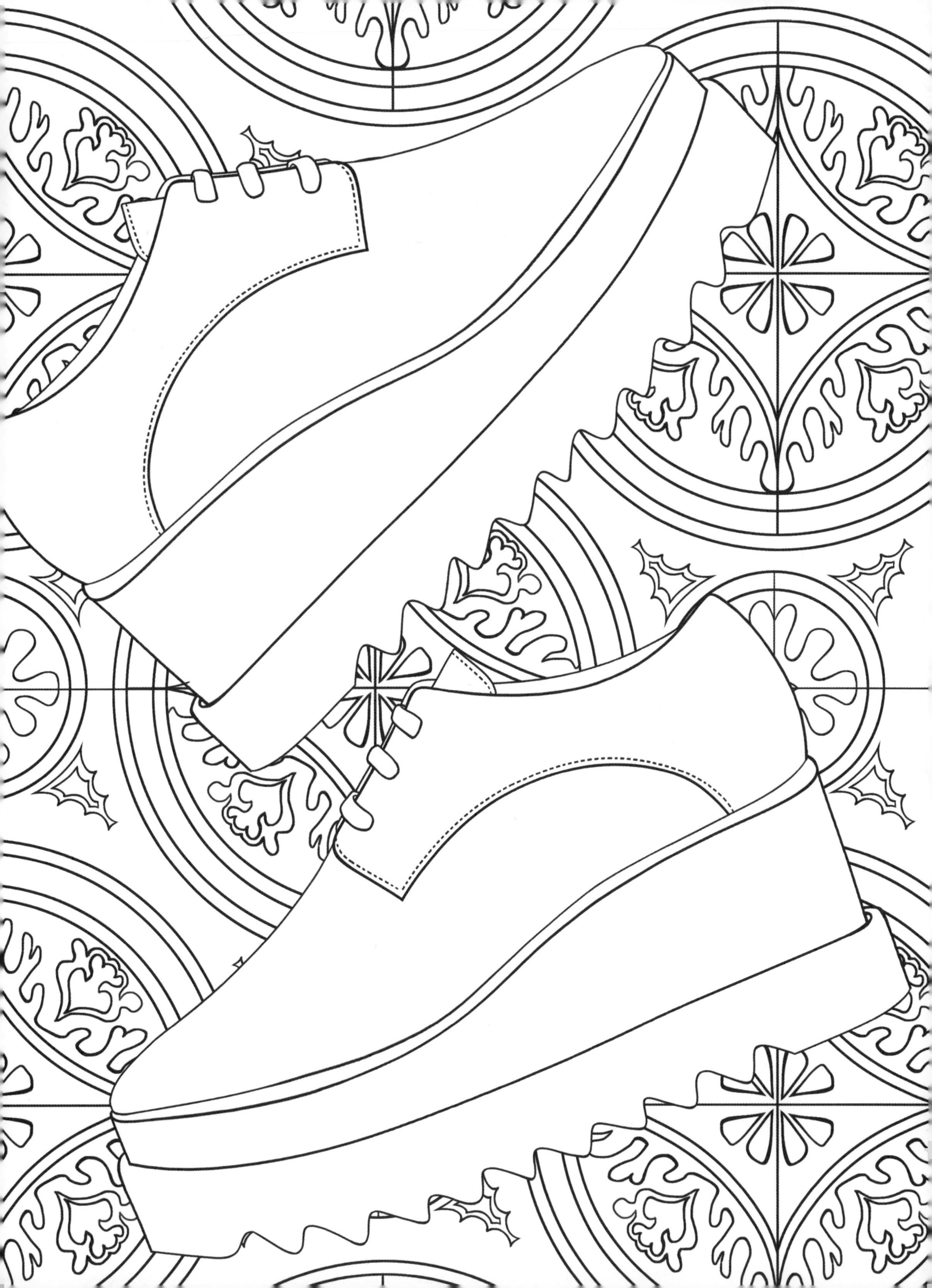

CHARLOTTE
Gainsbourg

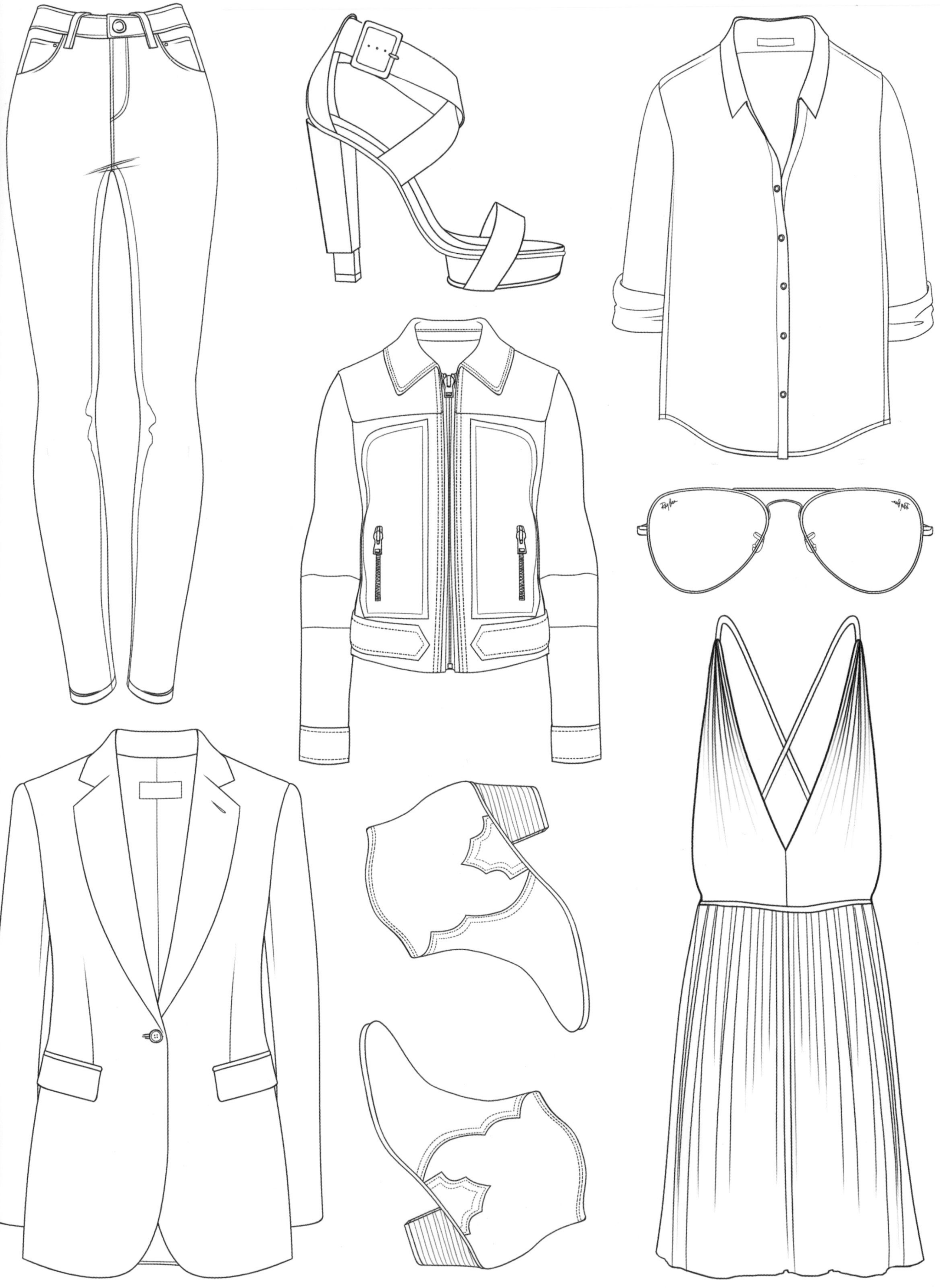

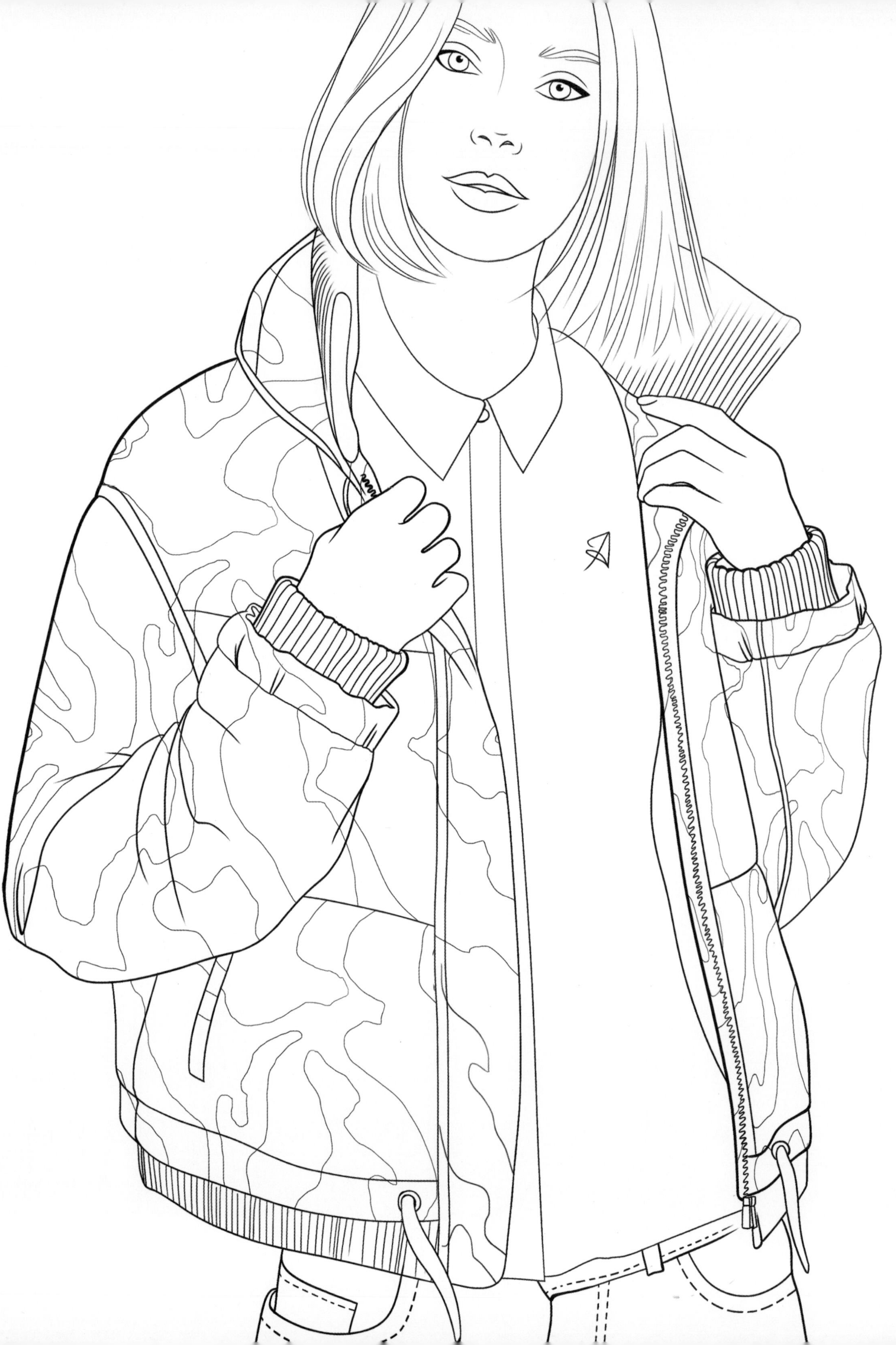

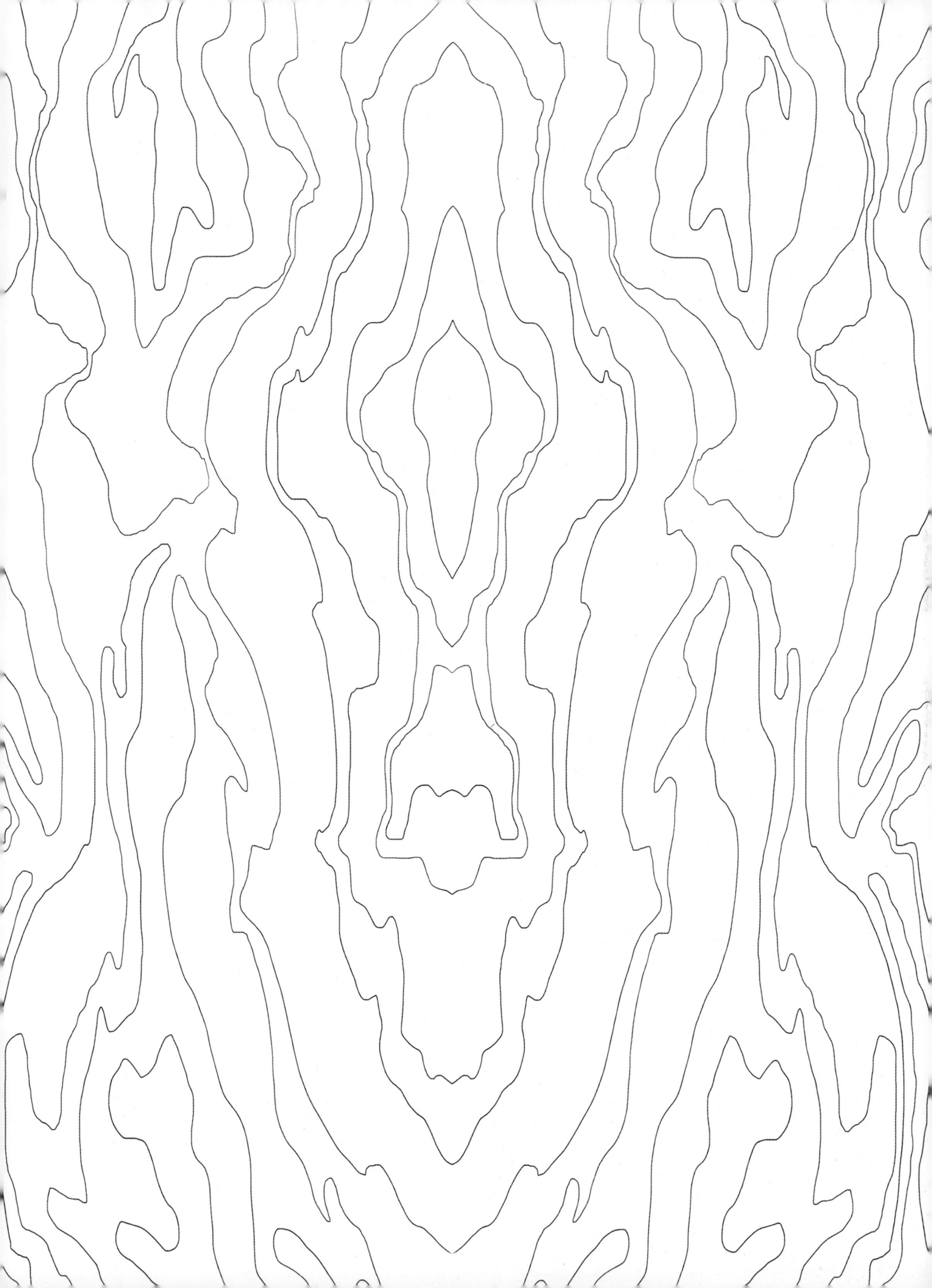

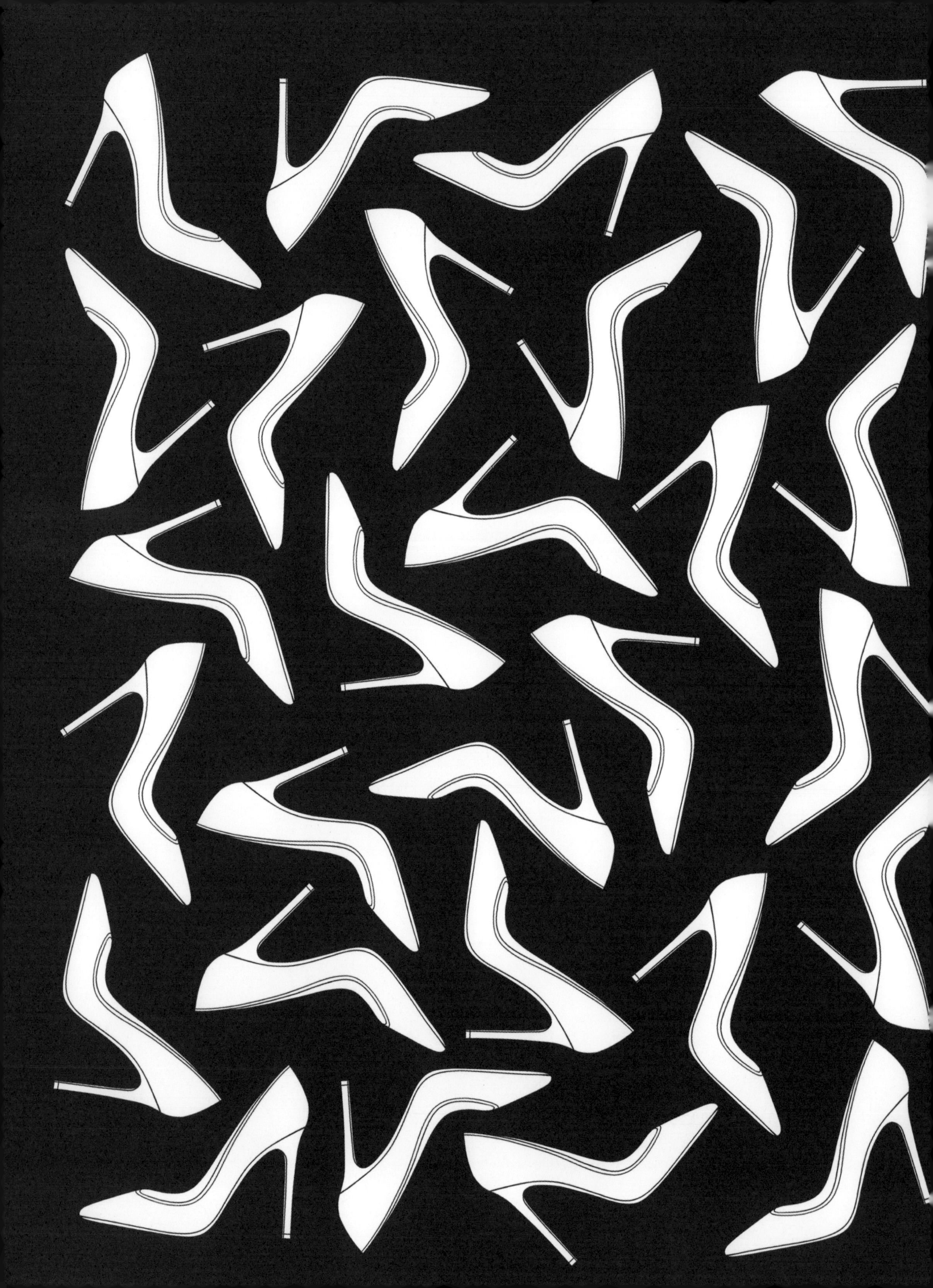

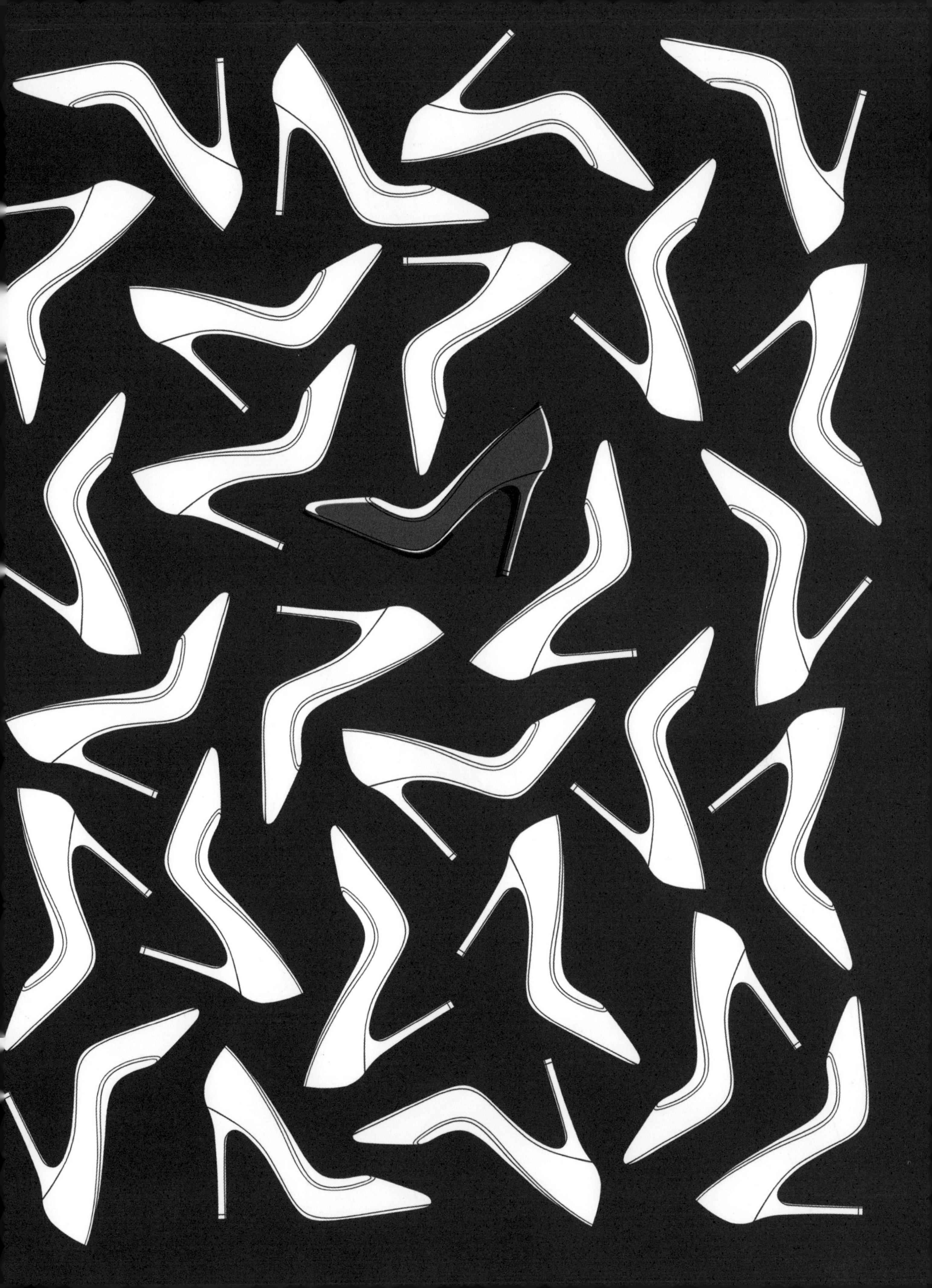

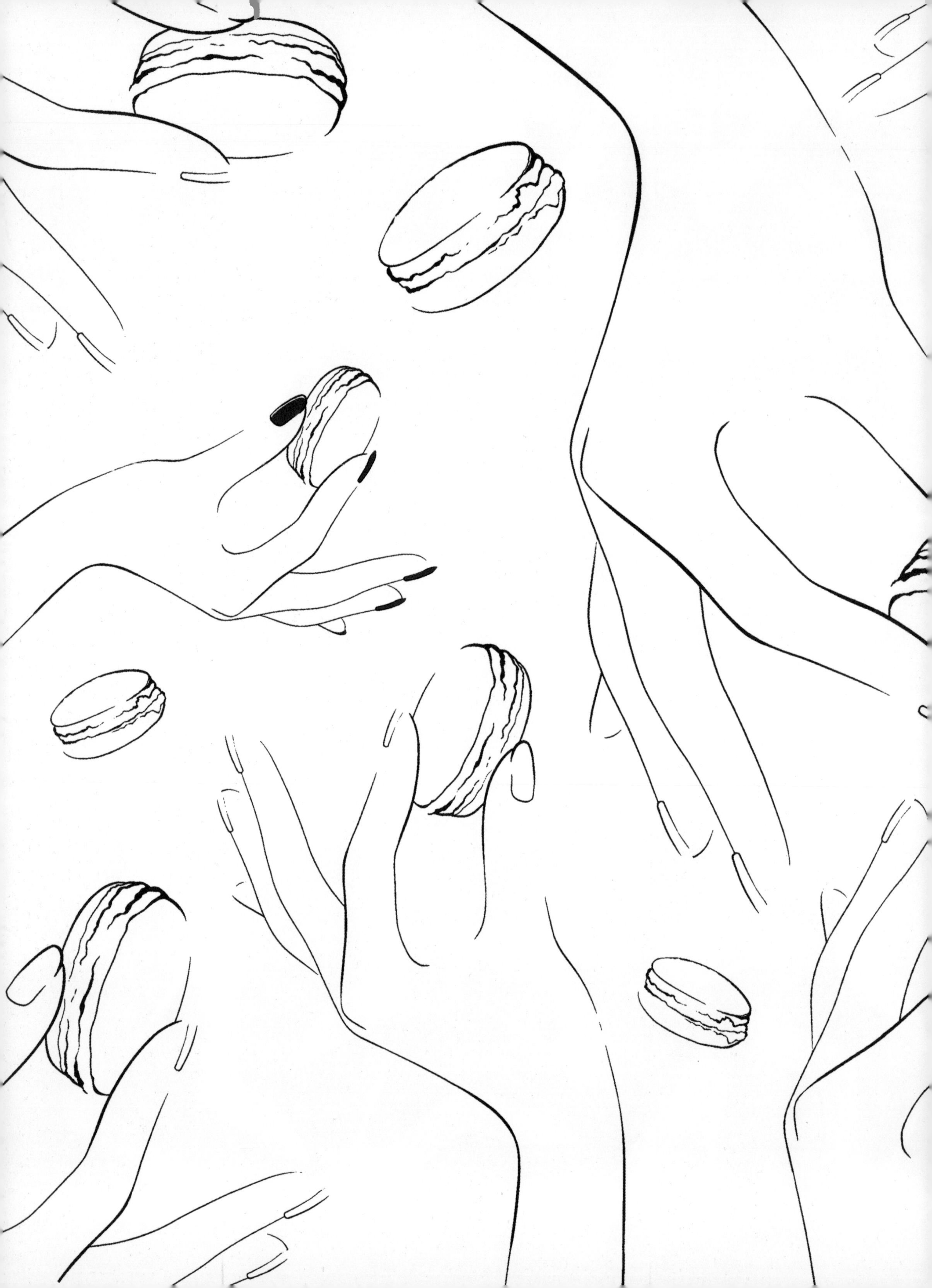

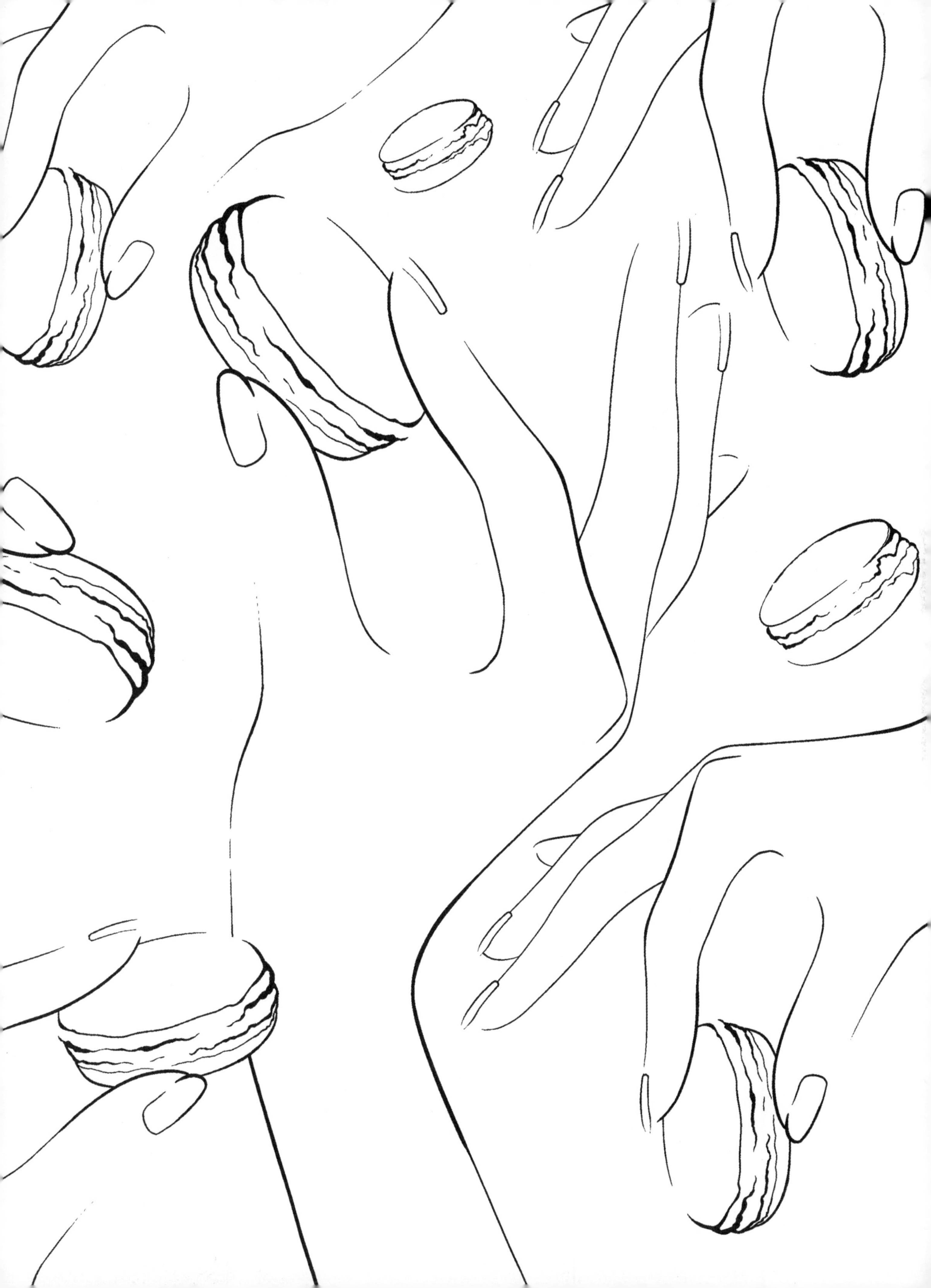

Le KIOSQUE

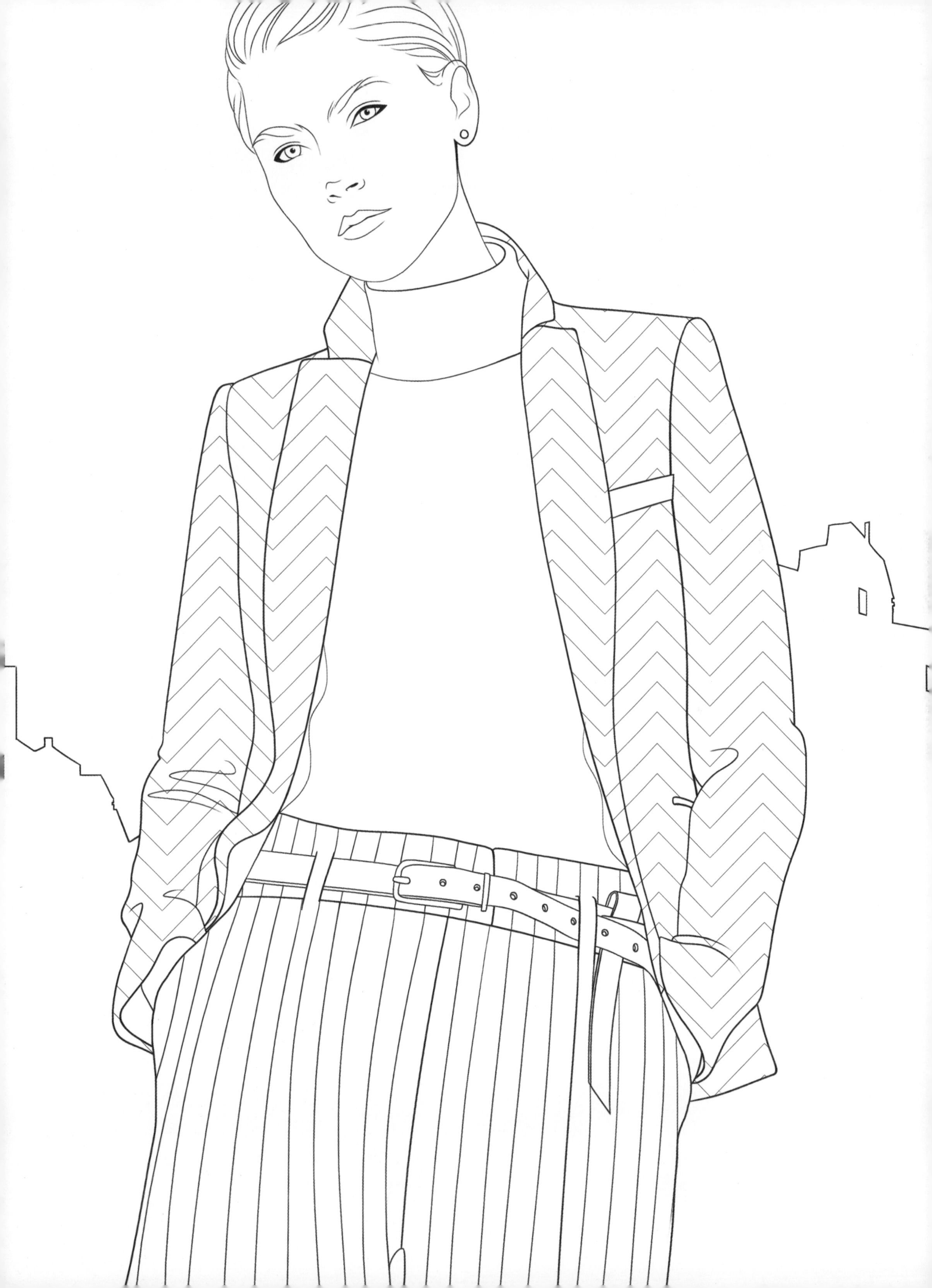

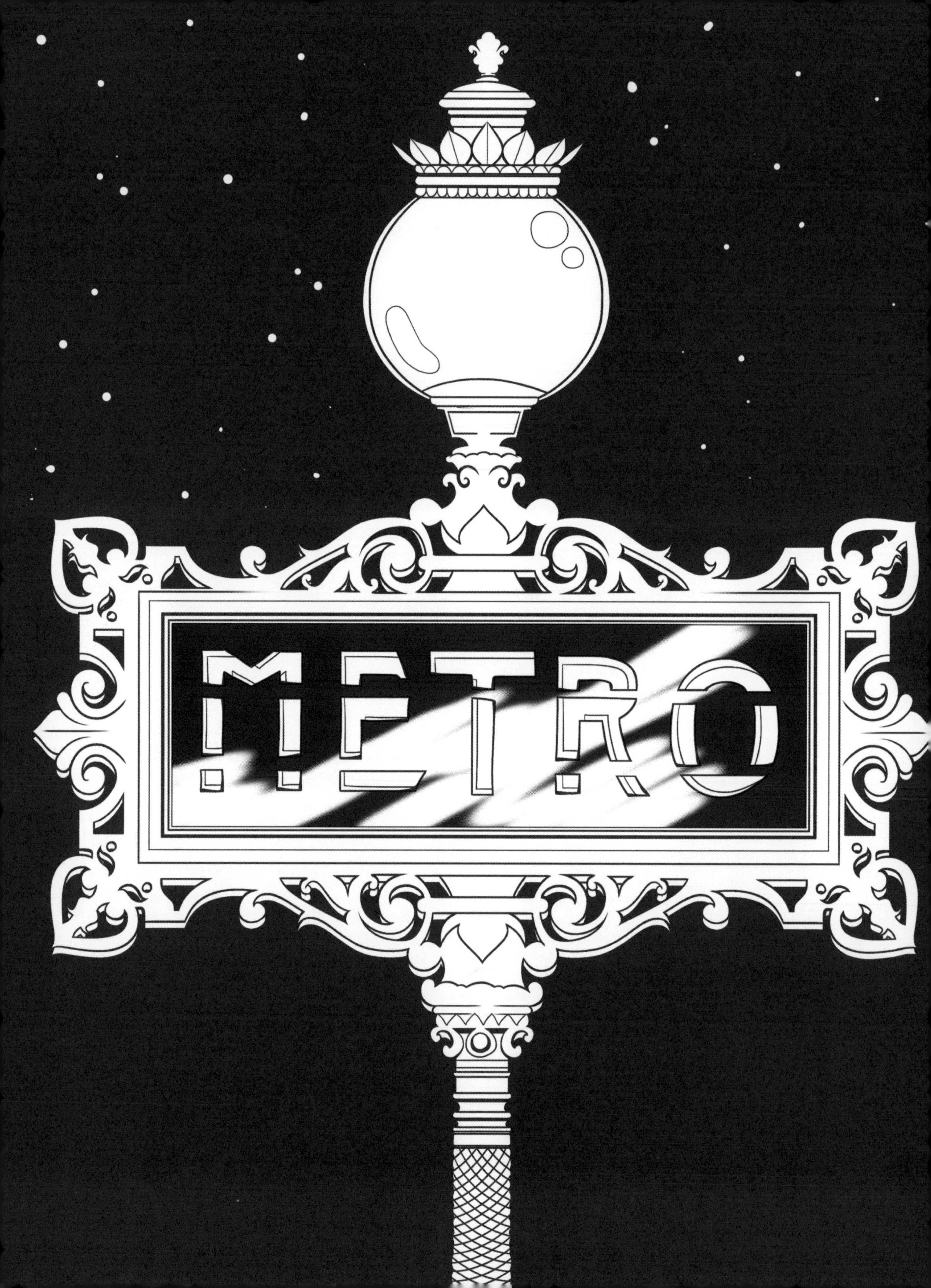
METRO

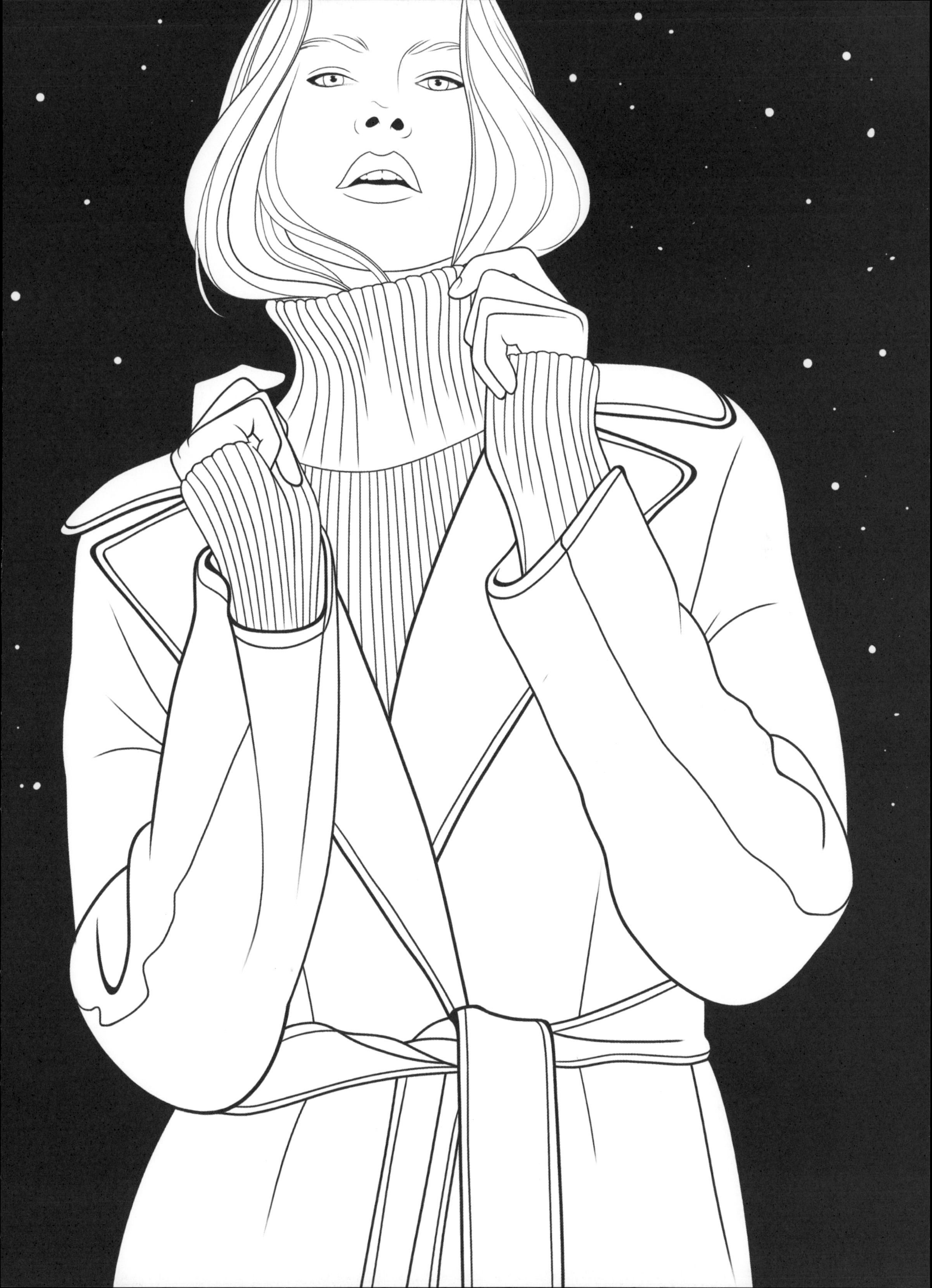

Maison fondée en 1862

LADURÉE

Paris

INDULGE IN GOURMET COLORS!

VANILLE	CAFÉ	MARRON	NOUGAT	PRALINÉ
FRAISE	FRAMBOISE	MYRTILLE	CASSIS	RÉGLISSE
MENTHE	CHOCOLAT	CARAMEL	NOIX DE COCO	CITRON
RAISIN	PÊCHE	LITCHI	VIOLETTE	PAIN D'ÉPICE
ORANGE	MANGUE	BANANE	POMME	JASMIN
ROSE	MANDARINE	ABRICOT	RHUBARBE	CERISE
PAMPLEMOUSSE	ORGEAT	MIRABELLE	OLIVE	CANNELLE

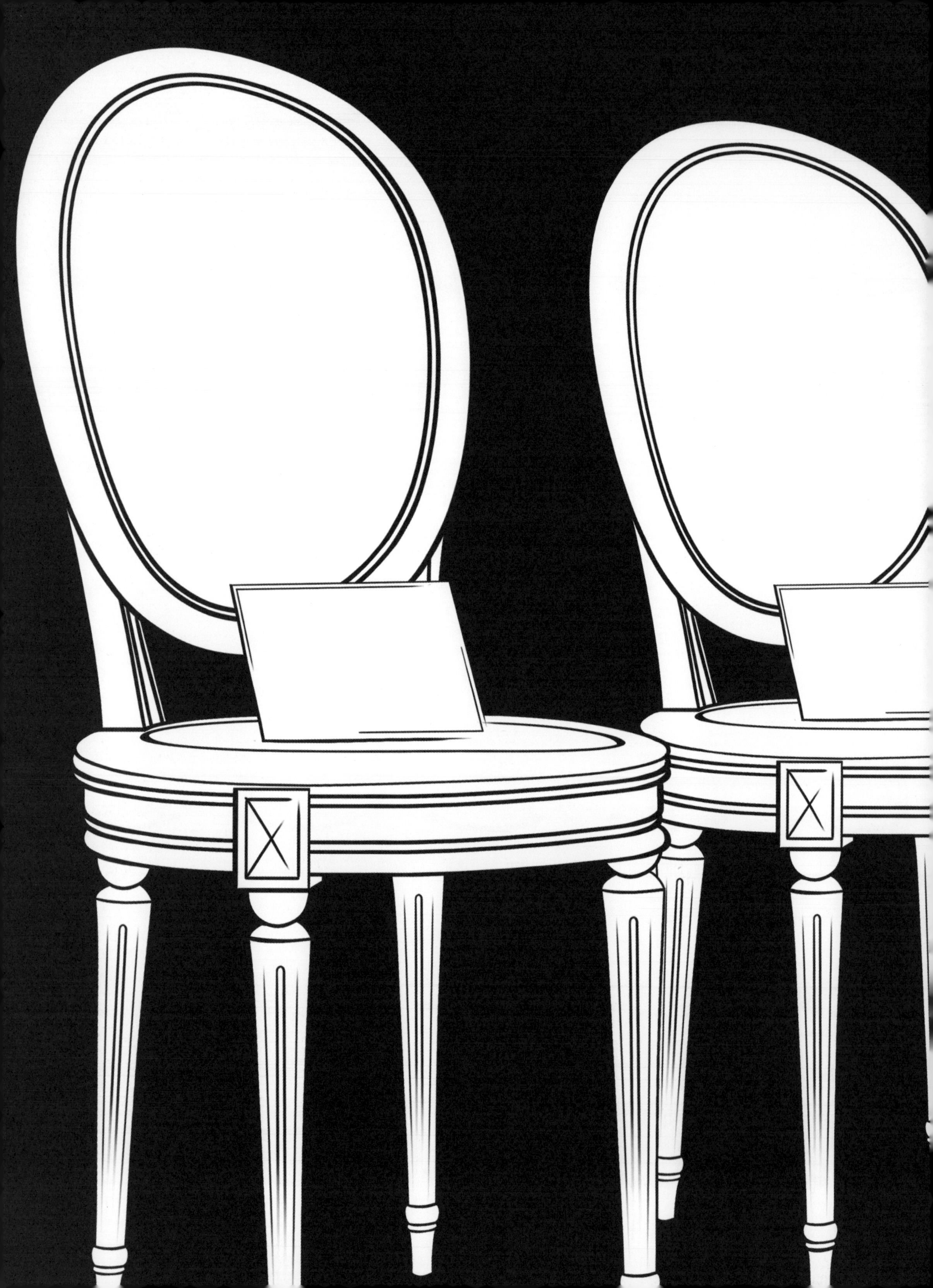

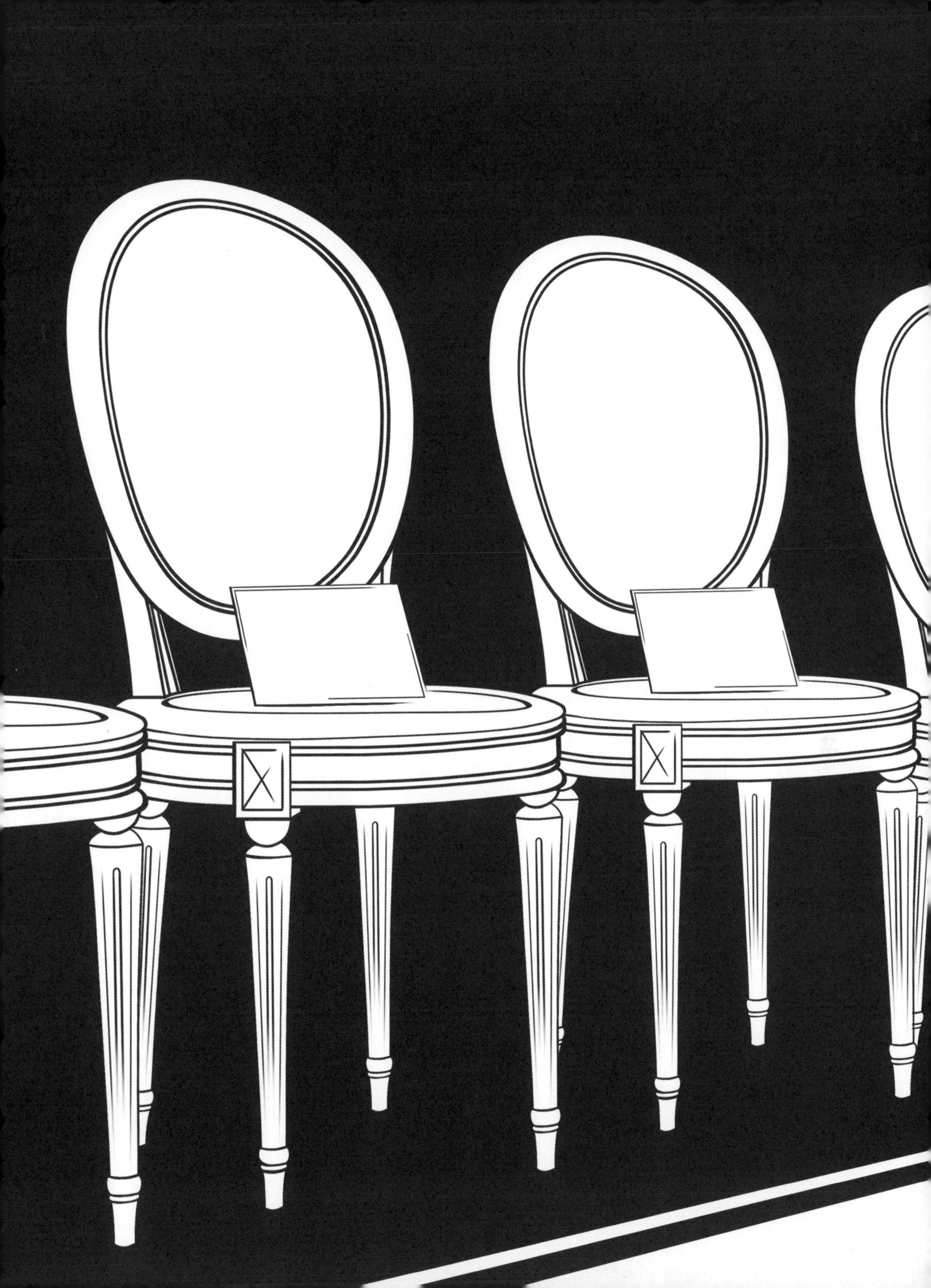

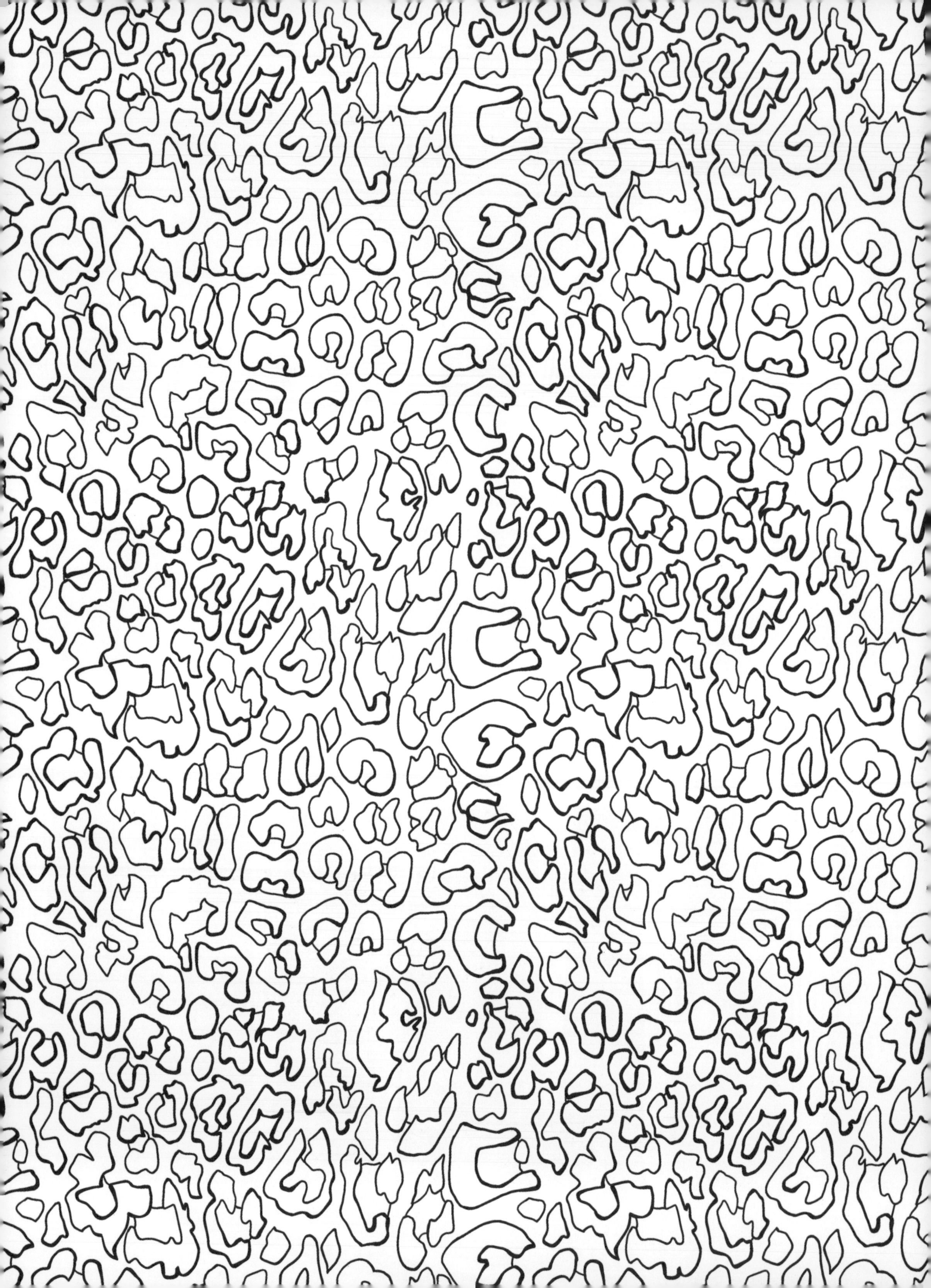

COLOR THE LEOPARD'S SPOTS

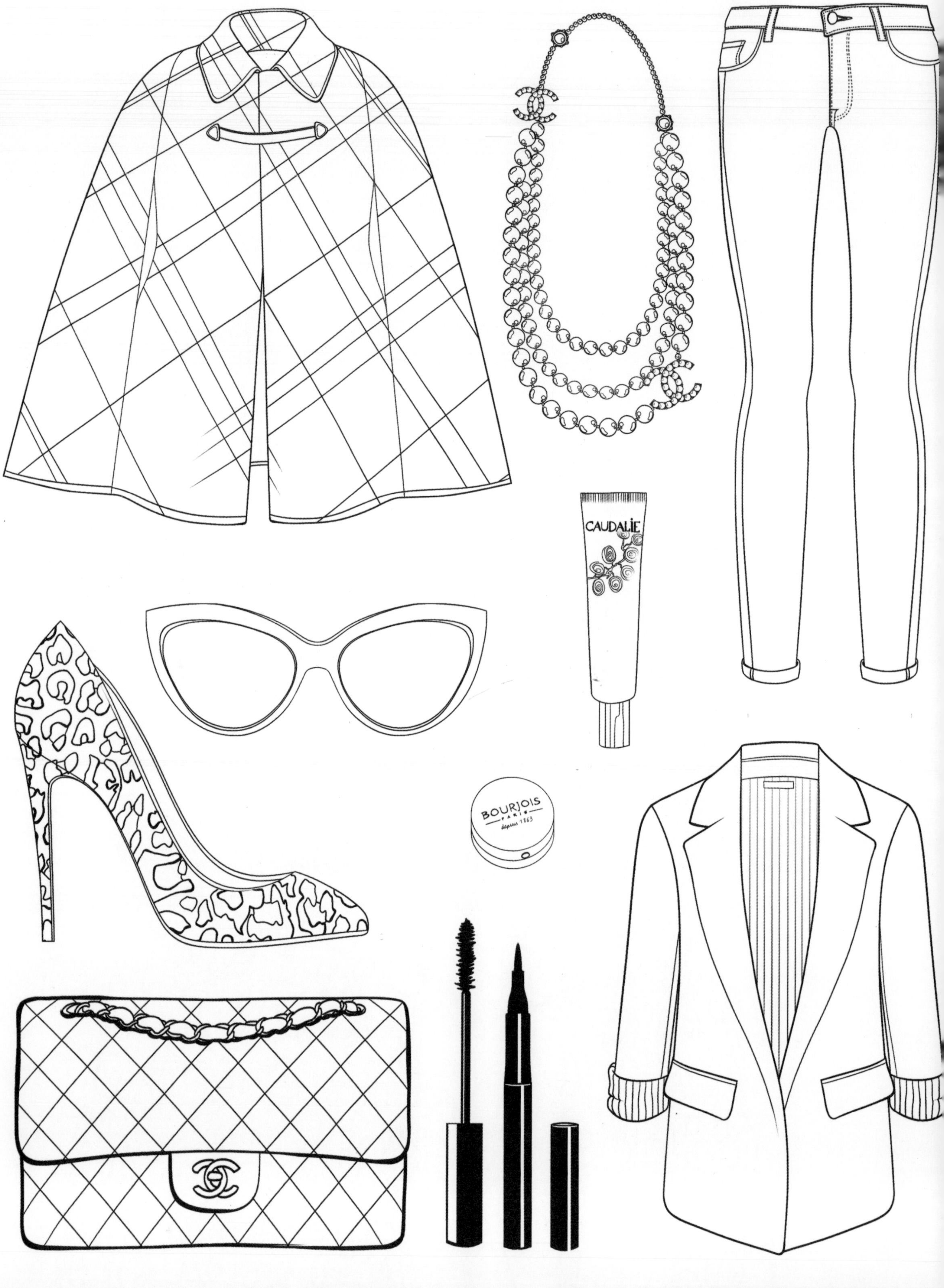
CAUDALIE
BOURJOIS
PARIS
depuis 1863

Ariane

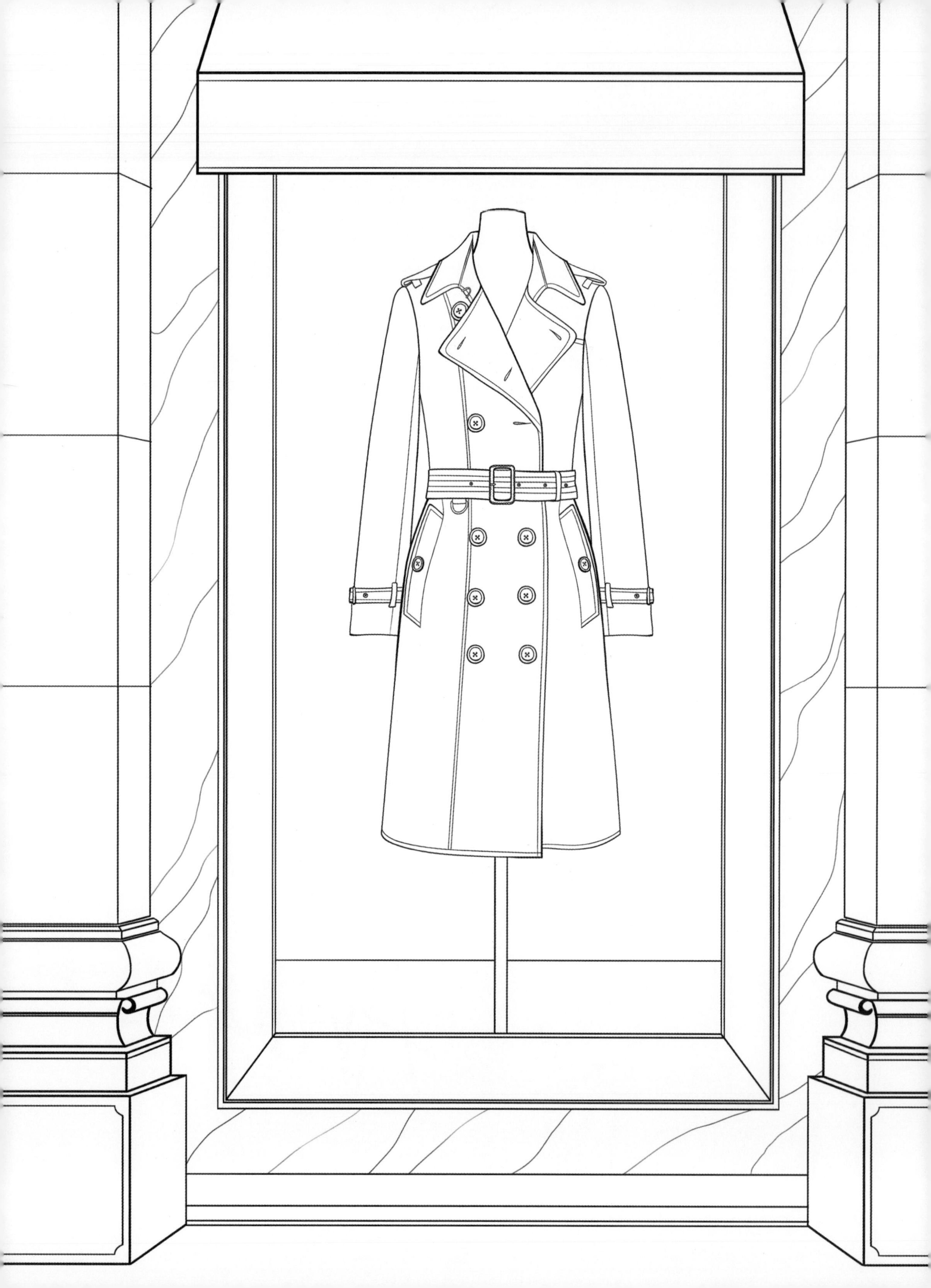

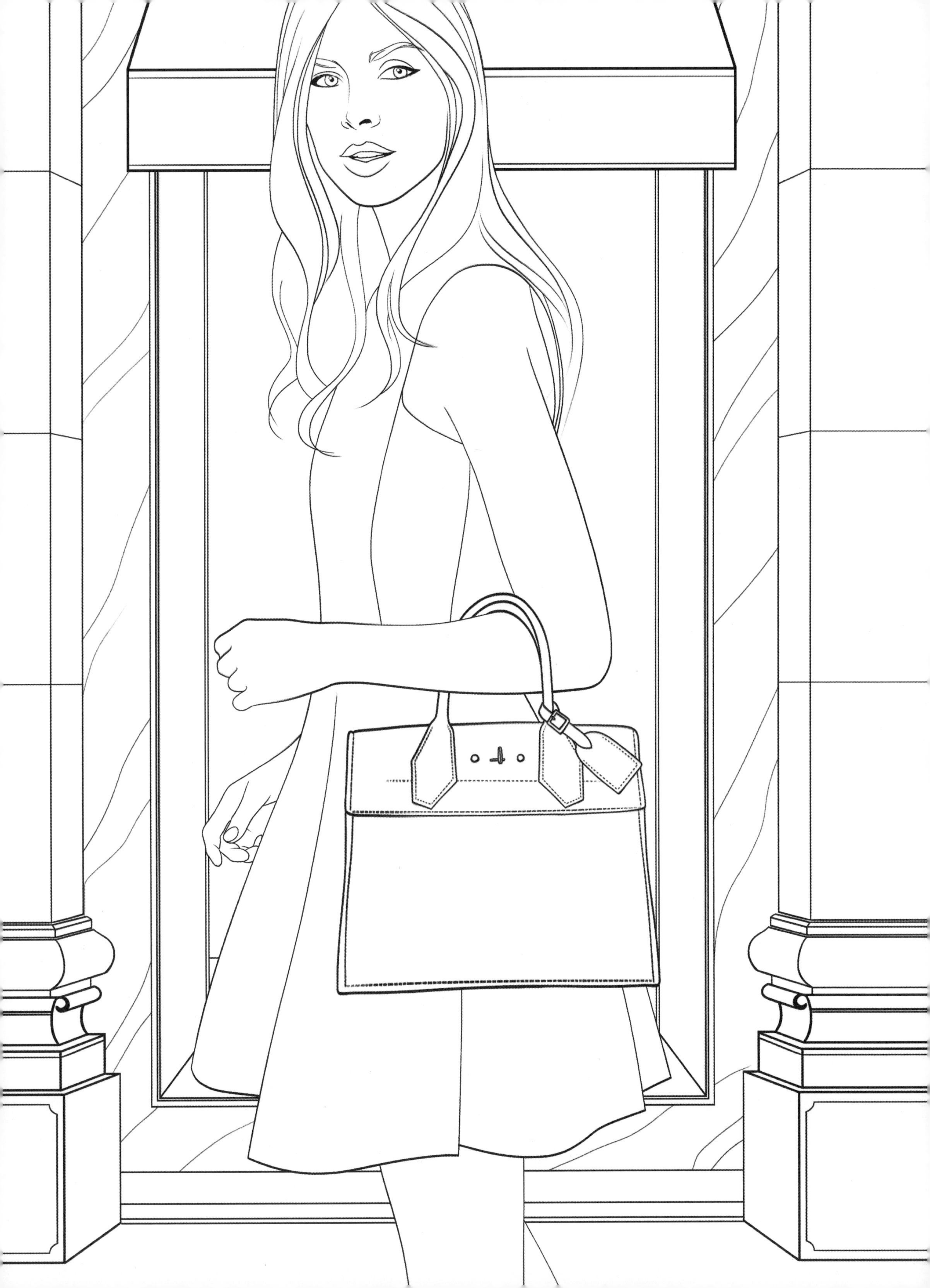

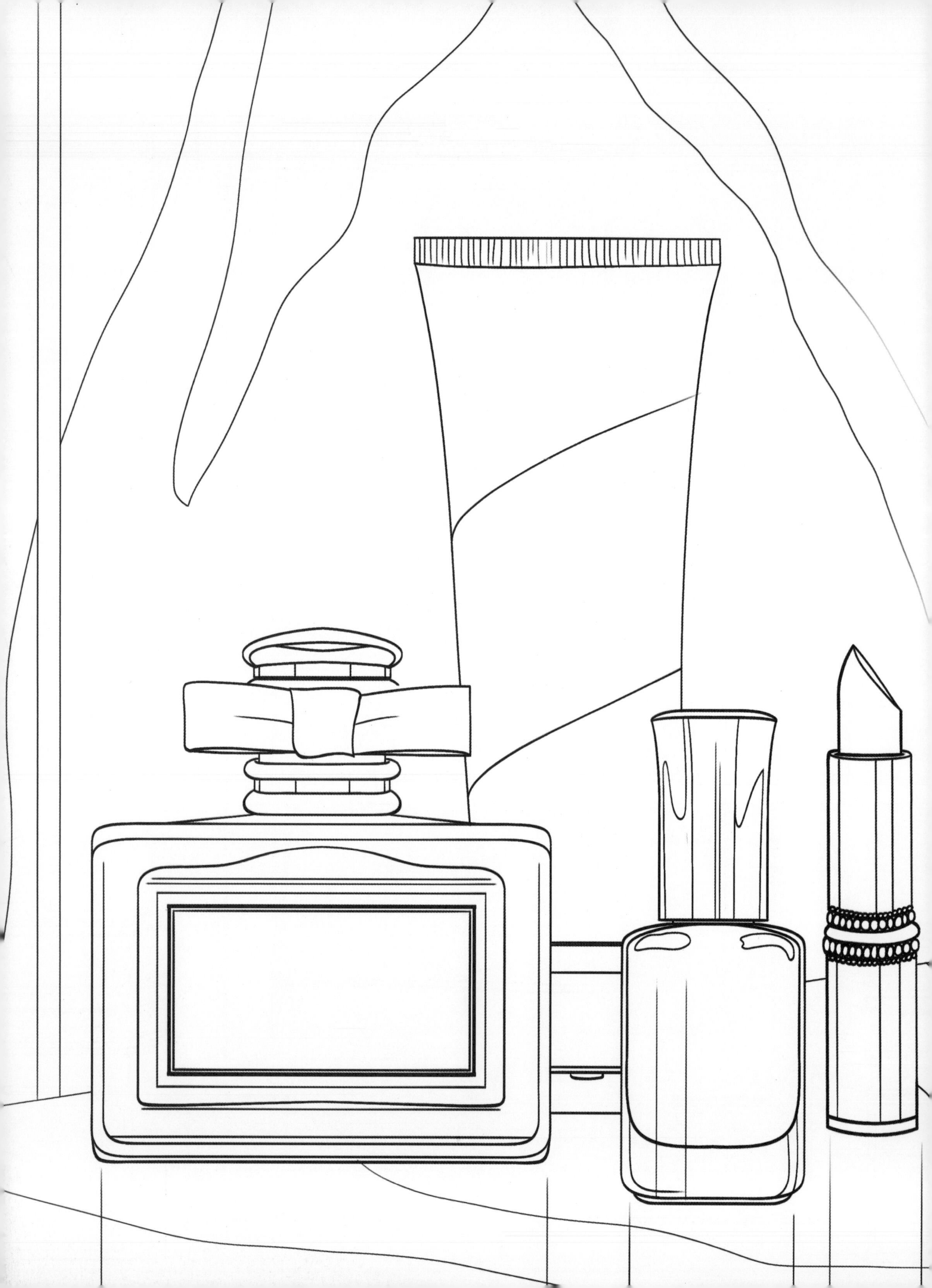

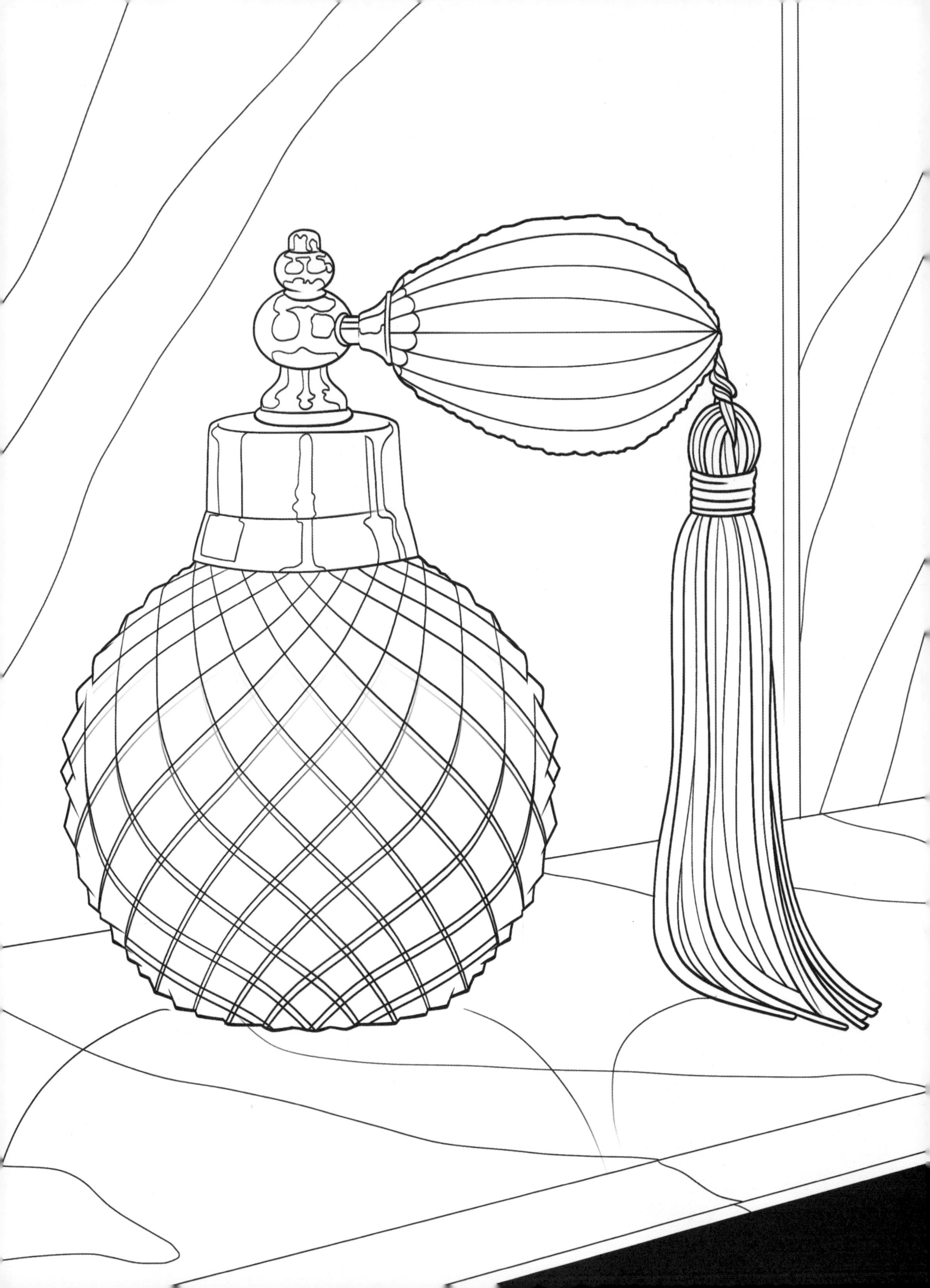

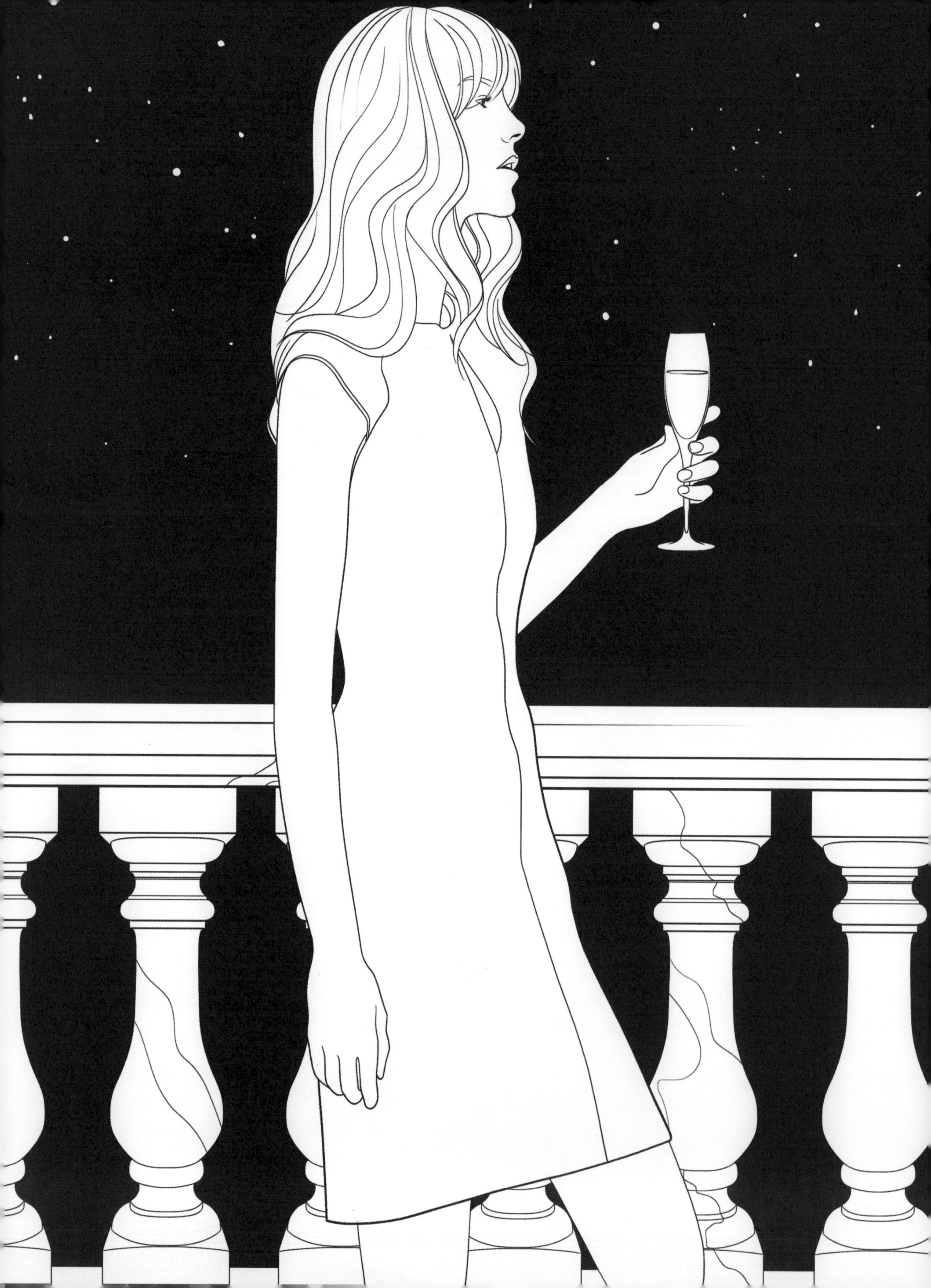

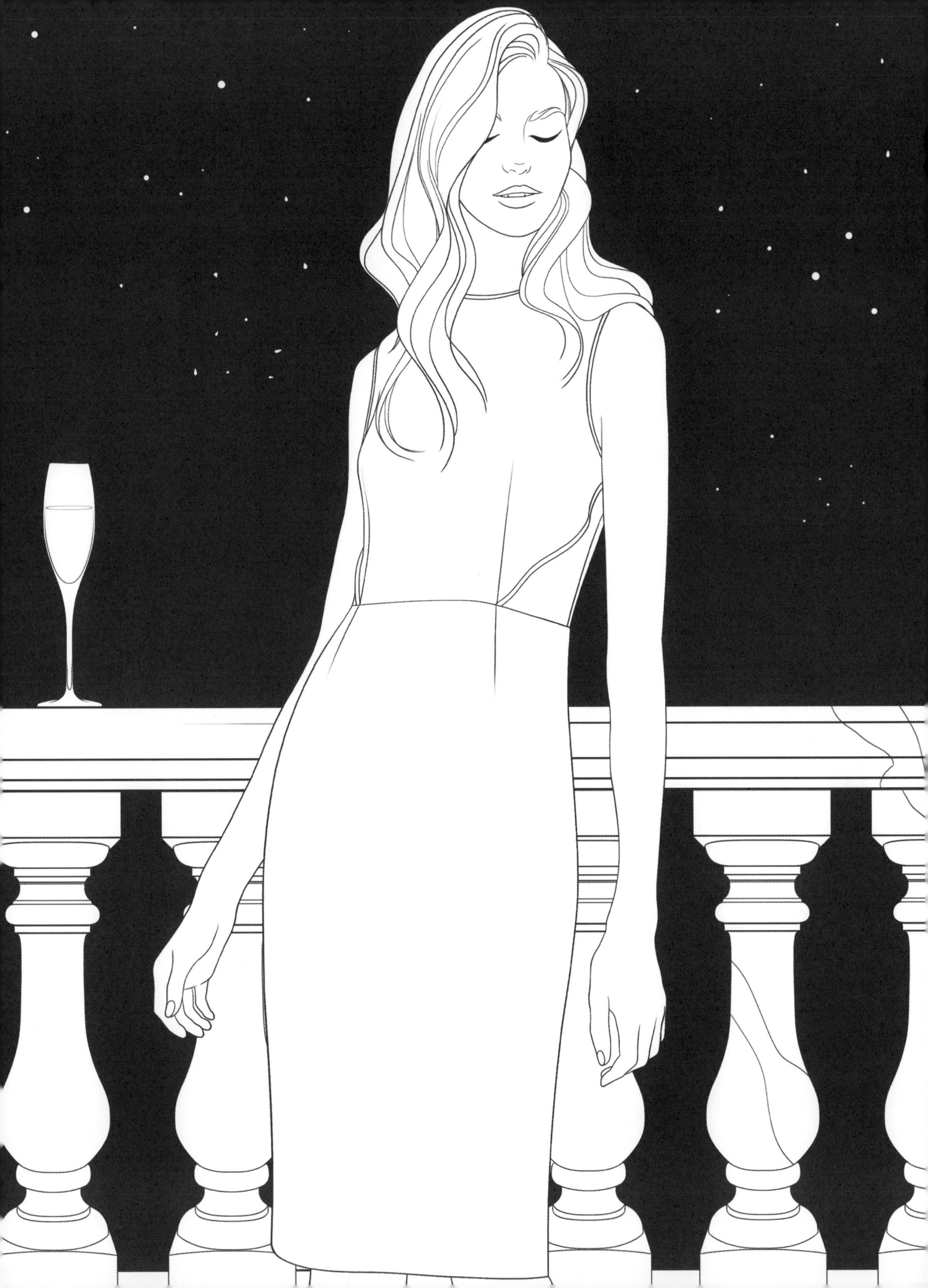

LES ESCARPINS

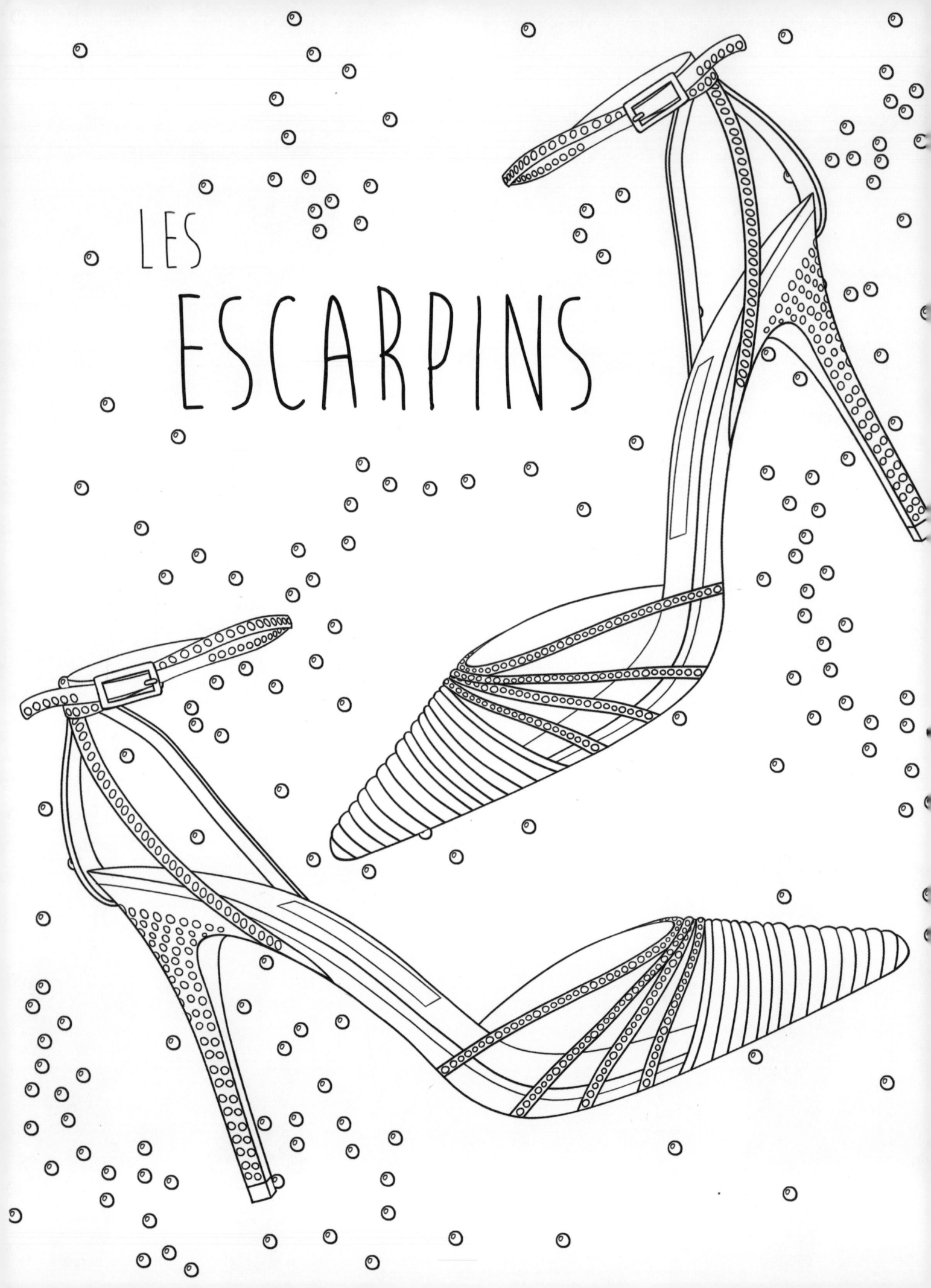

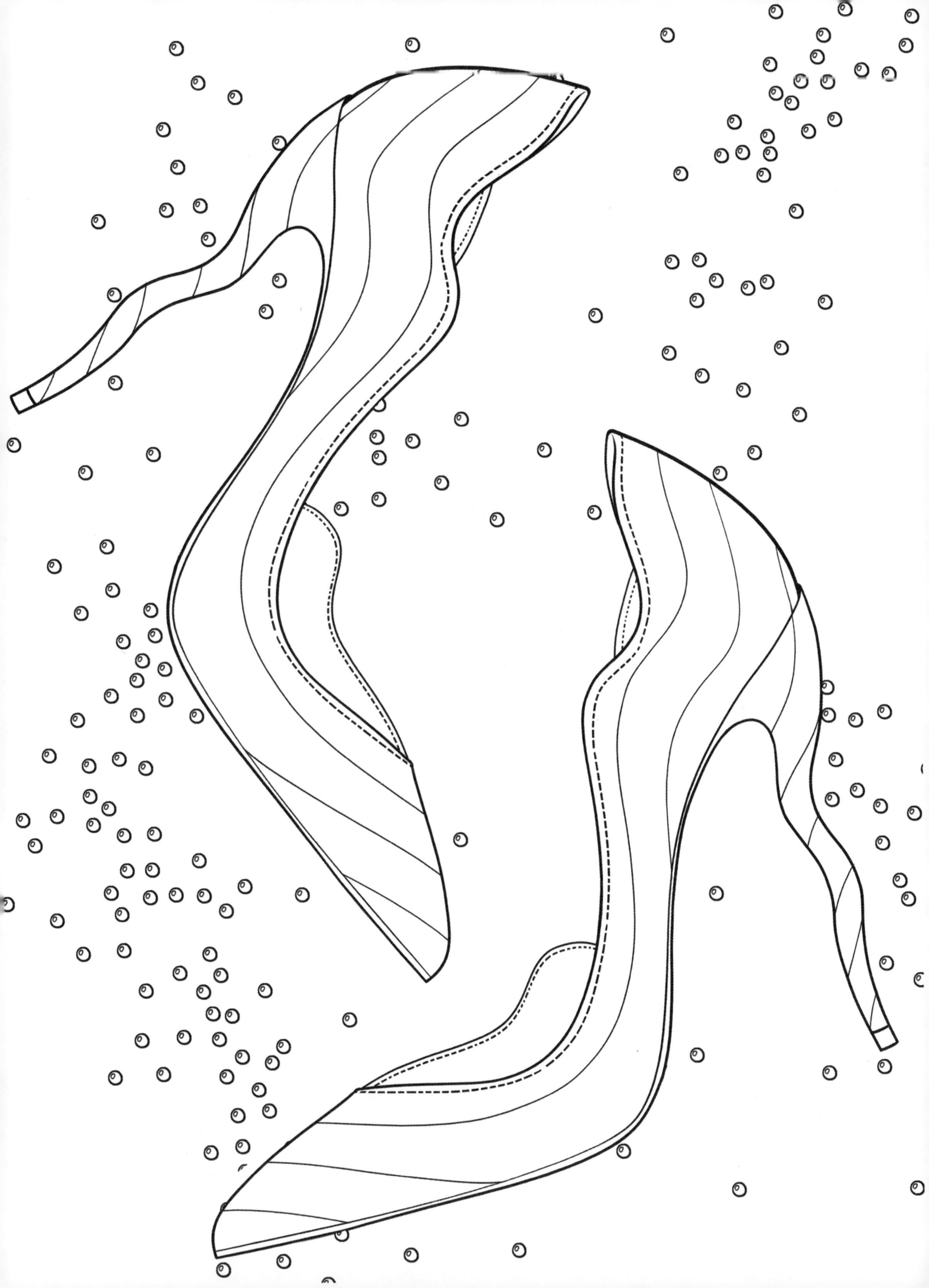

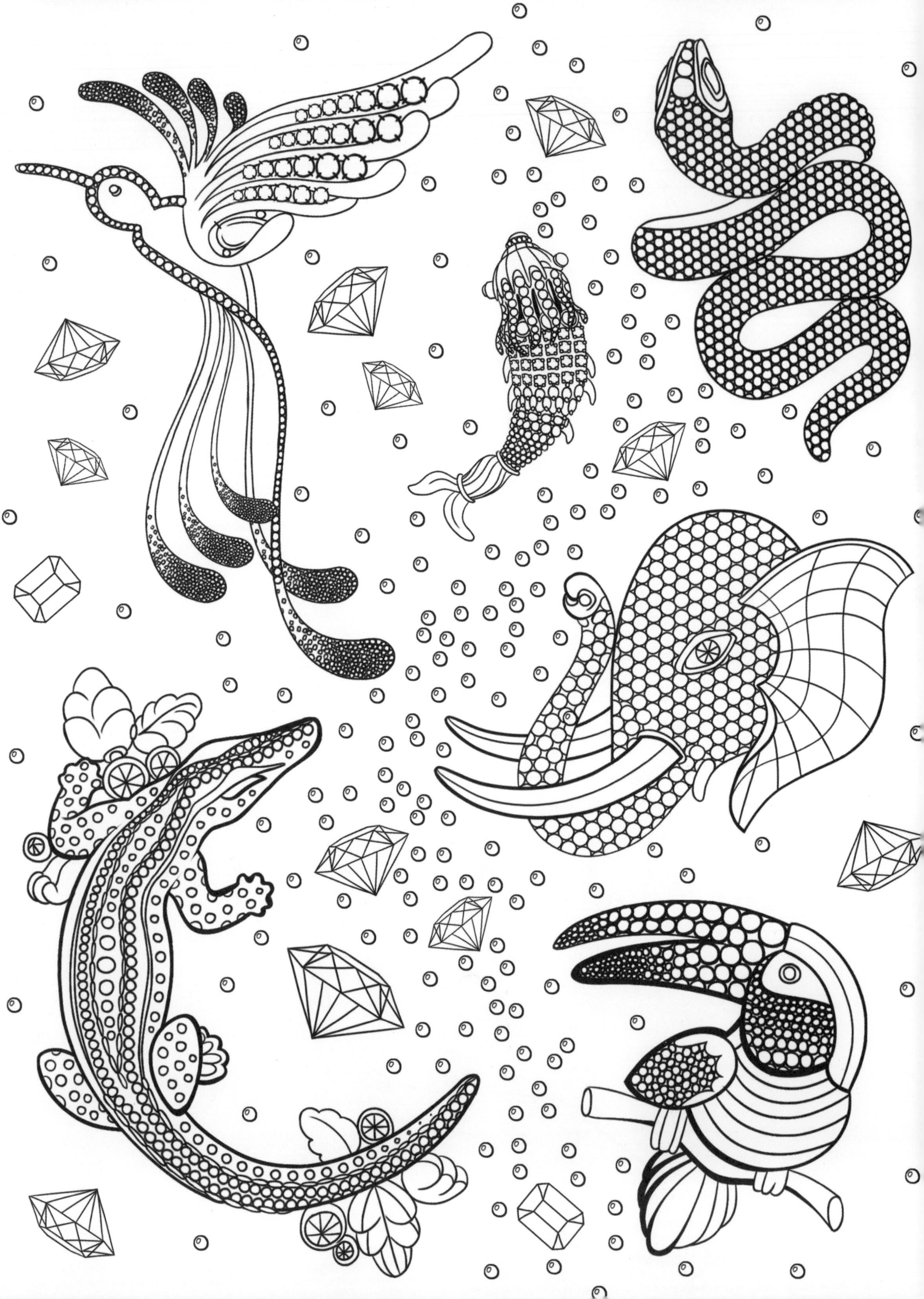

un Zoo place Vendôme

C'EST
LE PRINTEMPS...

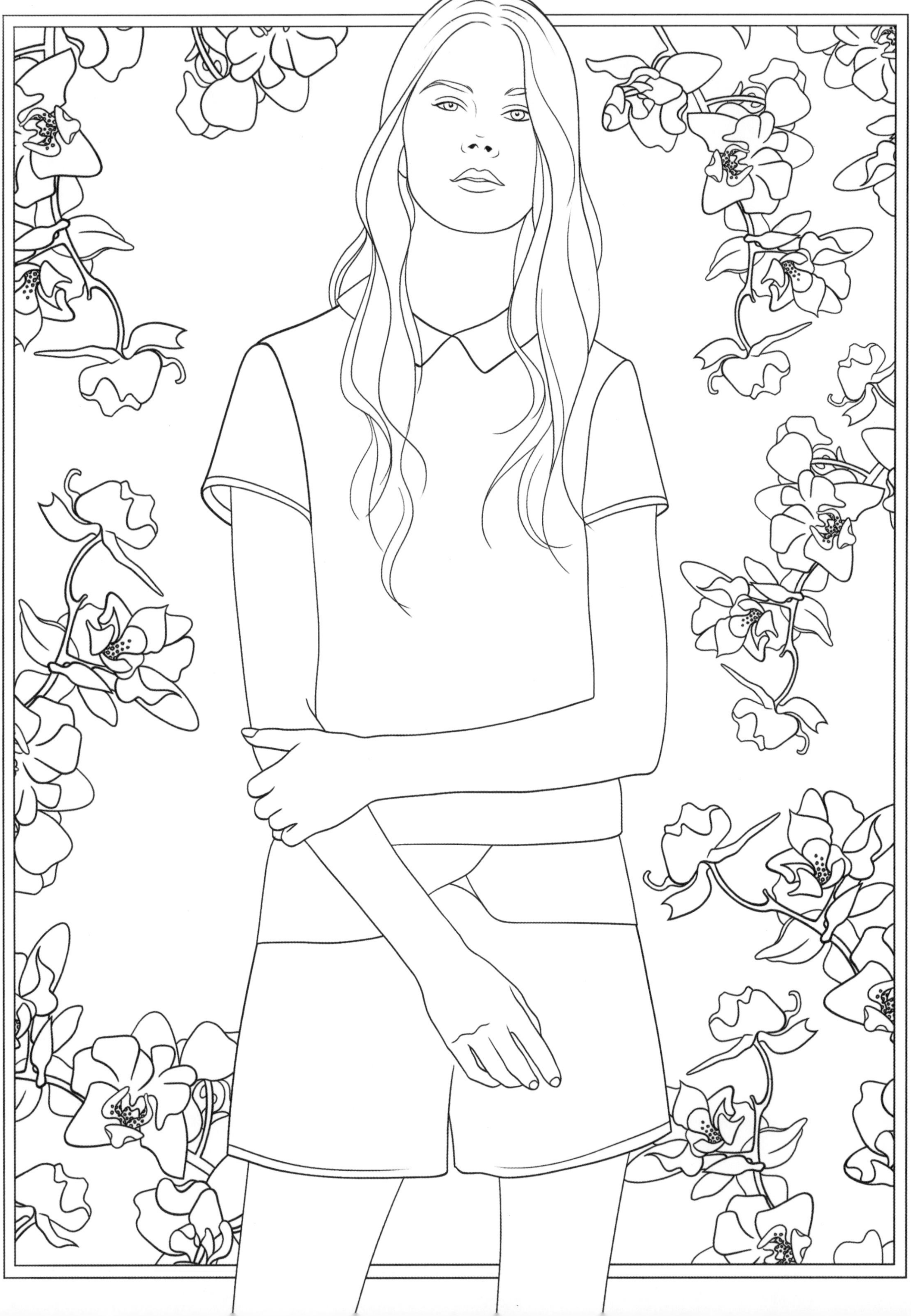

La marinière

Contrast your accessories with this classic sailor top

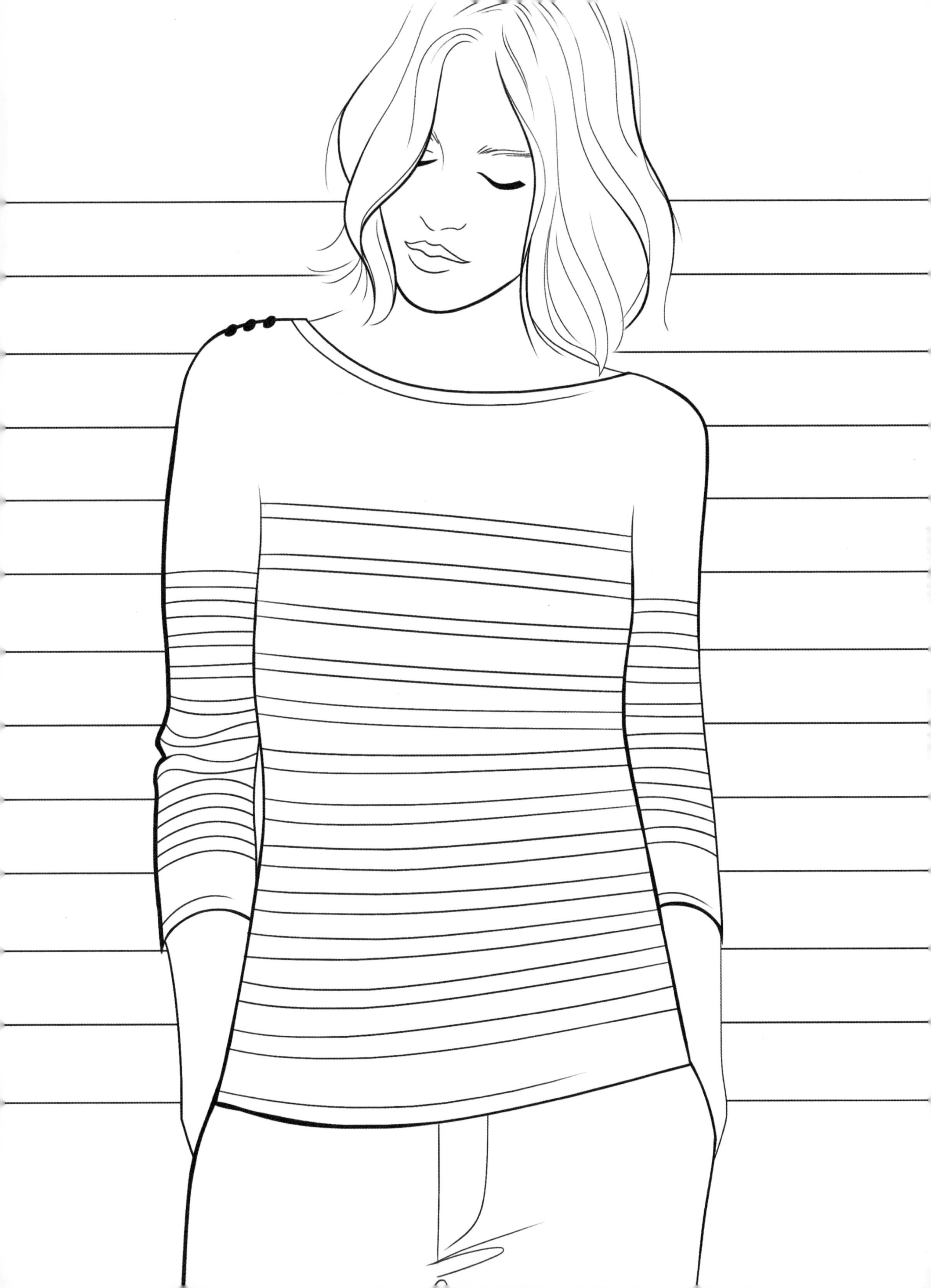

SNEAKERS
EN VILLE

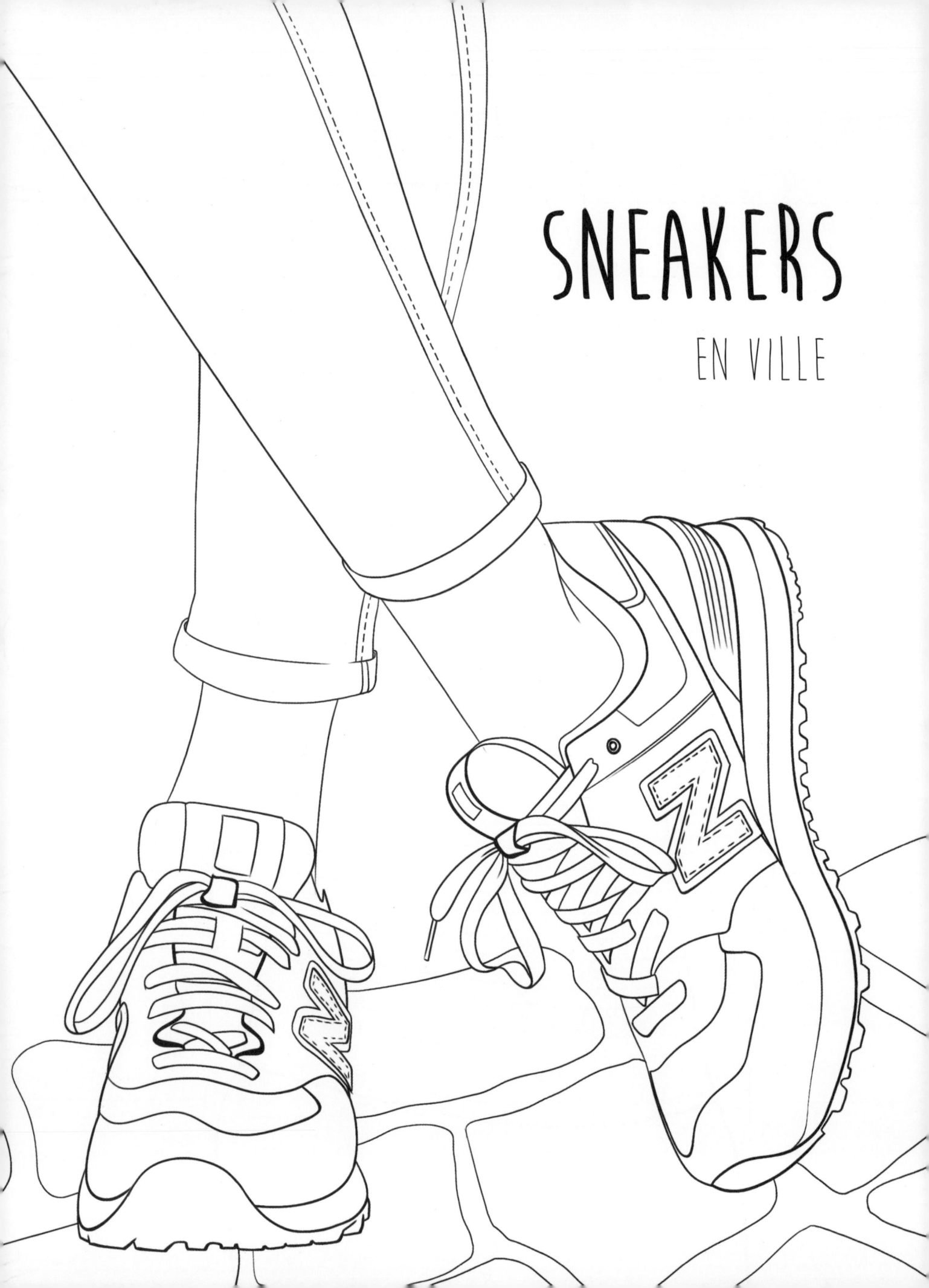

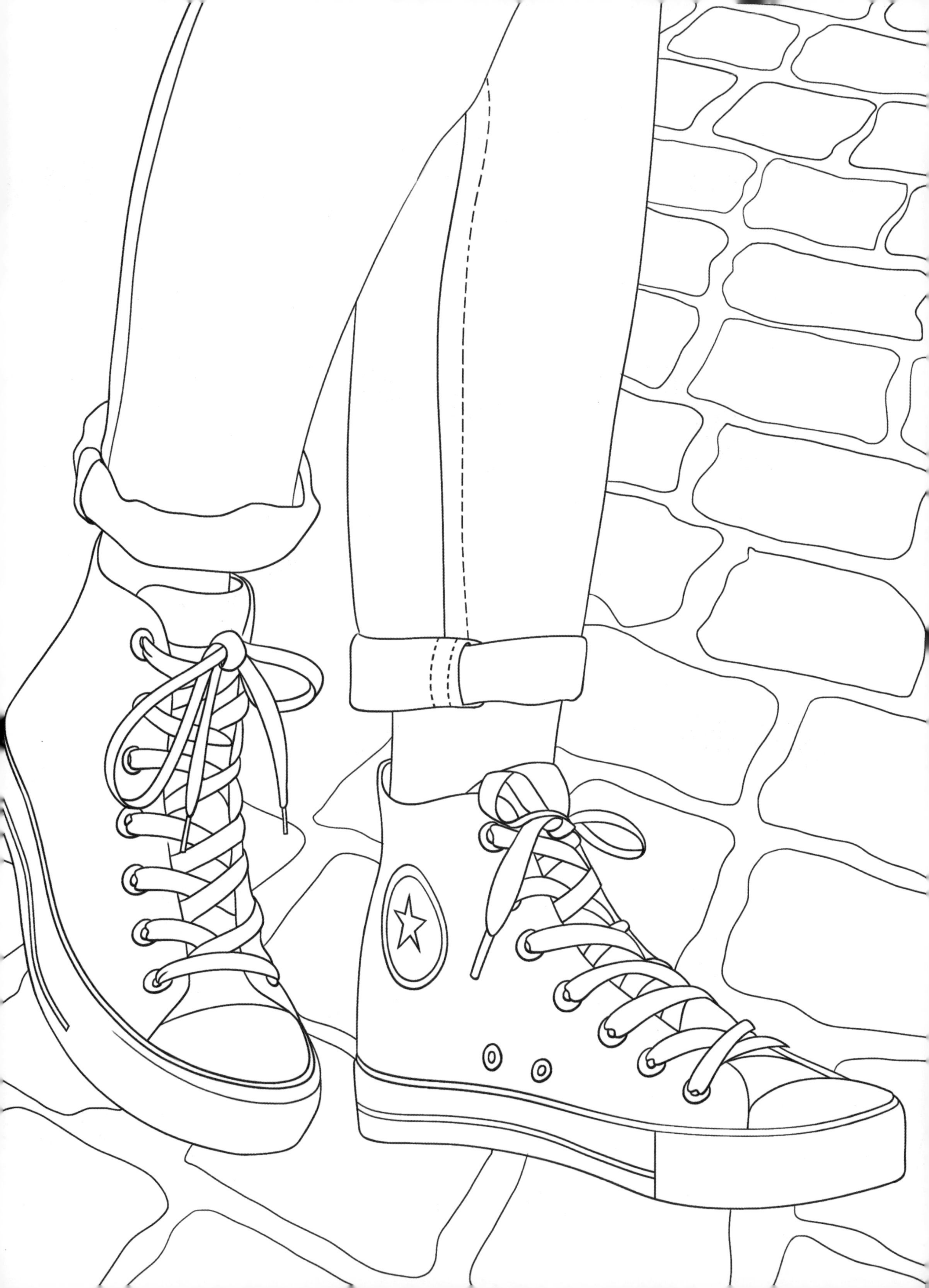

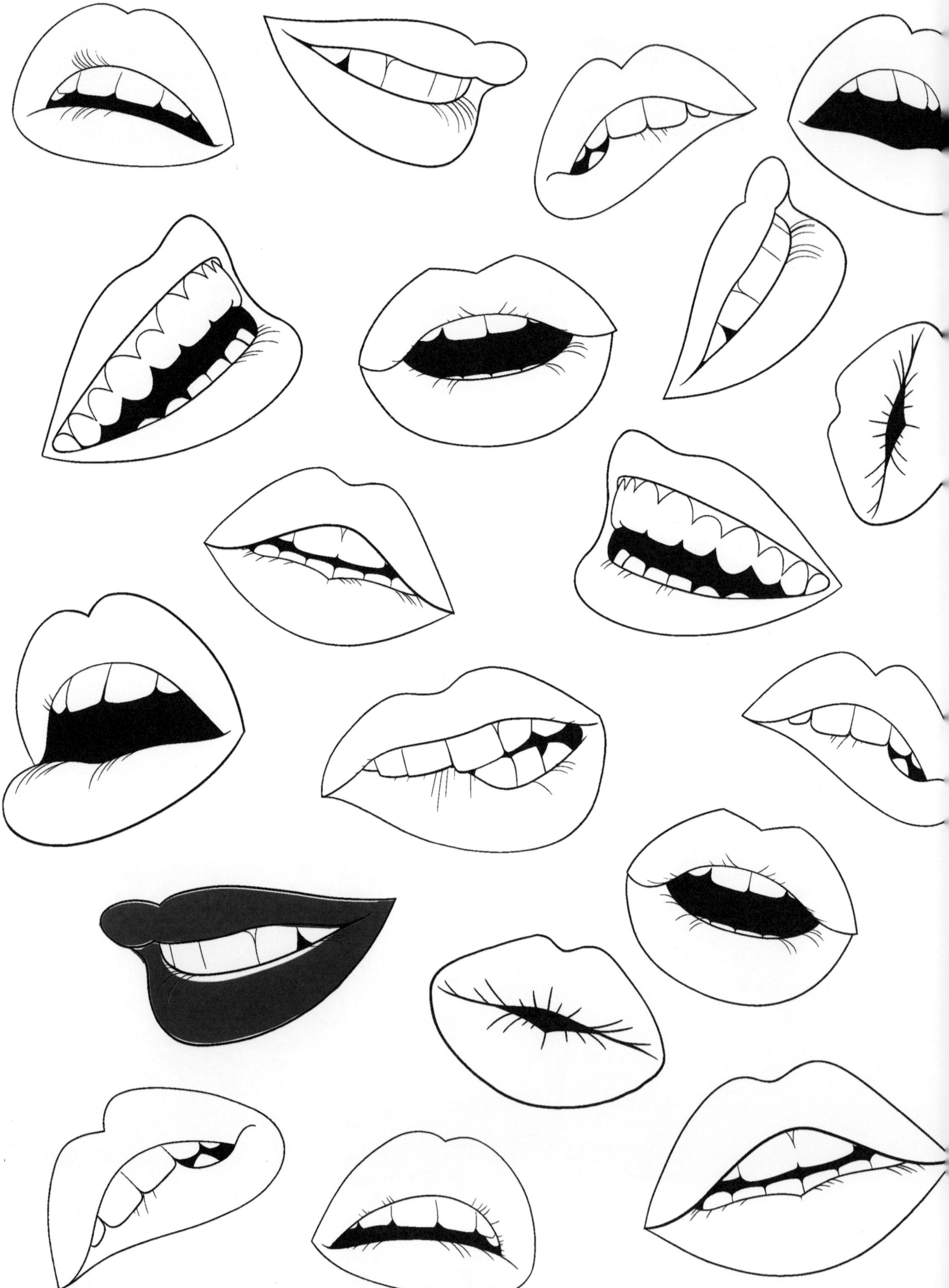

LA BOUCHE rouge

KISS ME!

LA BLOUSE EN SOIE

UPDATE THIS PRINT WITH BRILLIANT COLORS

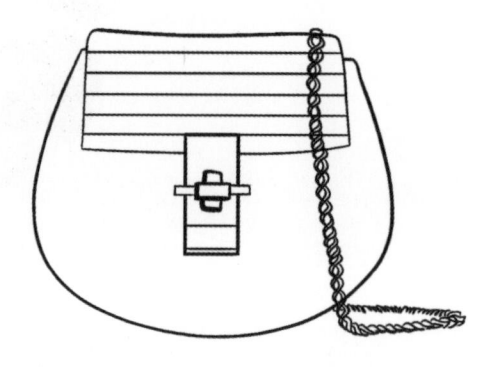

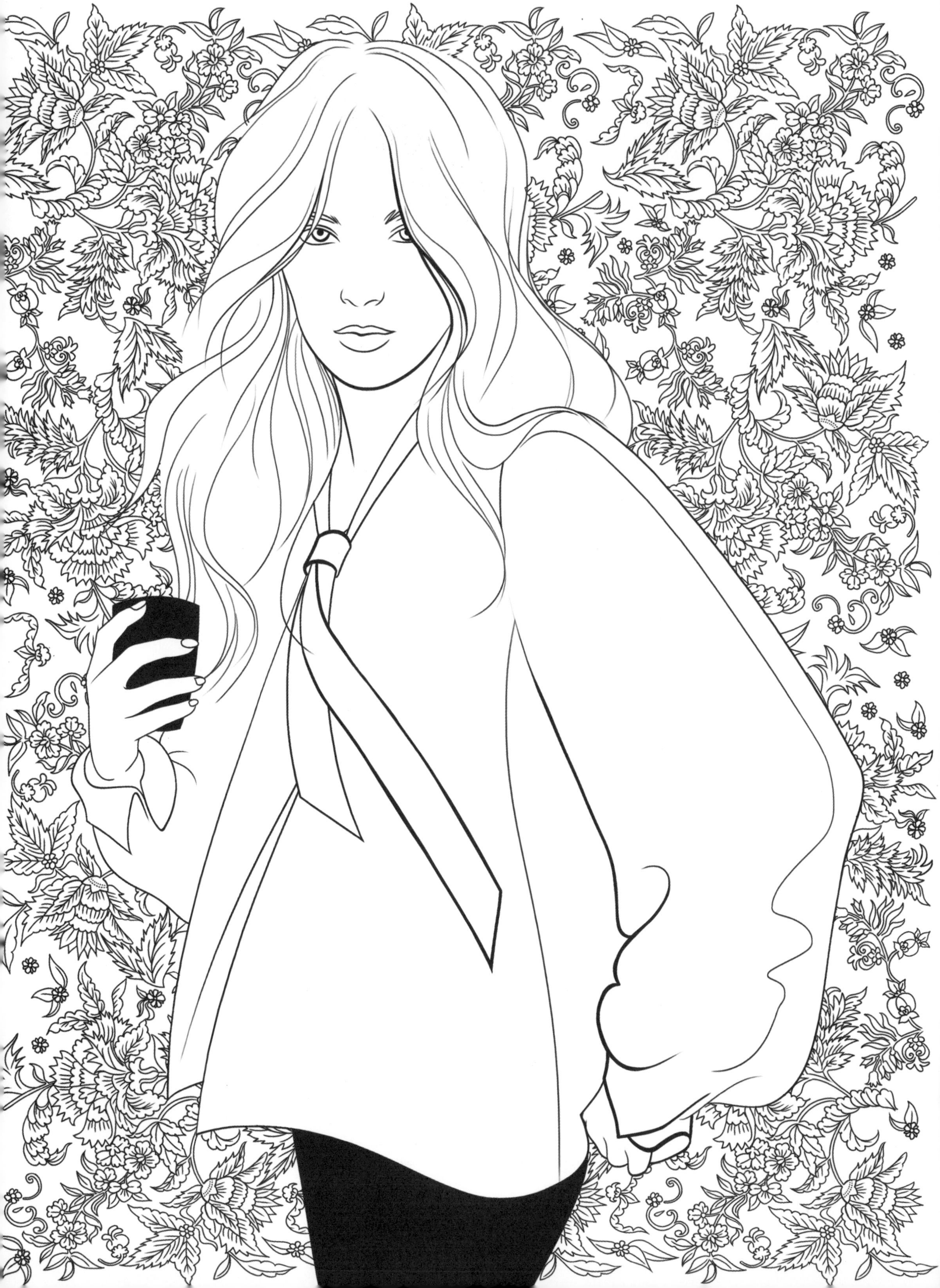

LE VERNIS

CHANEL

LE VERNIS
CHANEL
LE VERNIS
CHANEL
LE VERNIS
CHANEL
LE VERNIS
CHANEL
LE VERNIS
CHANEL
LE VERNIS
CHANEL
LE VERNIS
CHANEL
LE VERNIS
CHANEL
LE VERNIS
CHANEL
LE VERNIS
CHANEL
LE VERNIS
CHANEL
LE VERNIS
CHANEL
LE VERNIS
CHANEL
LE VERNIS
CHANEL
LE VERNIS
CHANEL
LE VERNIS
CHANEL
LE VERNIS
CHANEL
LE VERNIS
CHANEL
LE VERNIS
CHANEL
LE VERNIS
CHANEL
LE VERNIS
CHANEL
LE VERNIS
CHANEL
LE VERNIS
CHANEL
LE VERNIS
CHANEL

JANE BIRKIN

SERGE GAINSBOURG — histoire de melody nelson

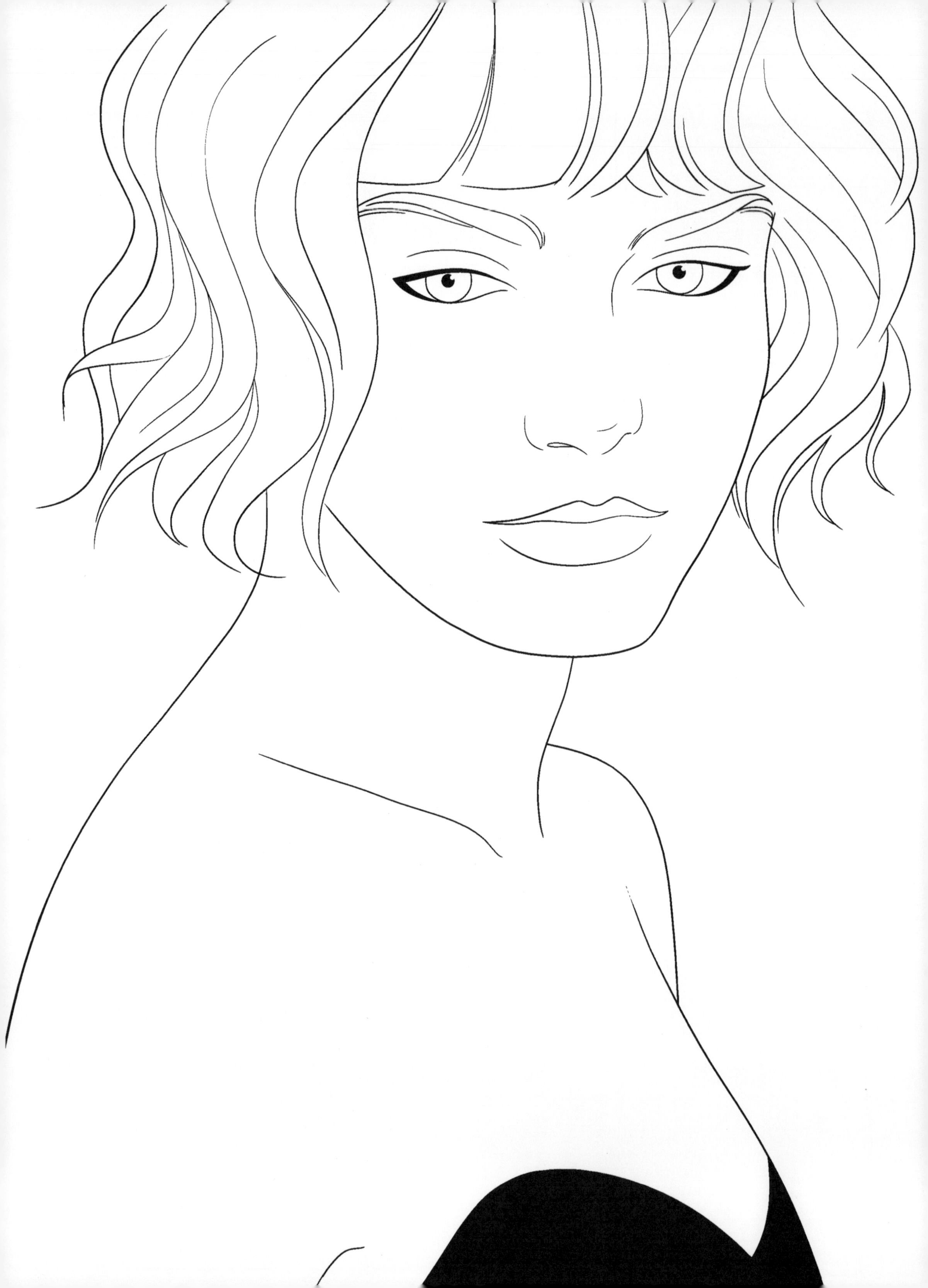

Grand Soir

PUT ON YOUR DREAMIEST

MAKEUP

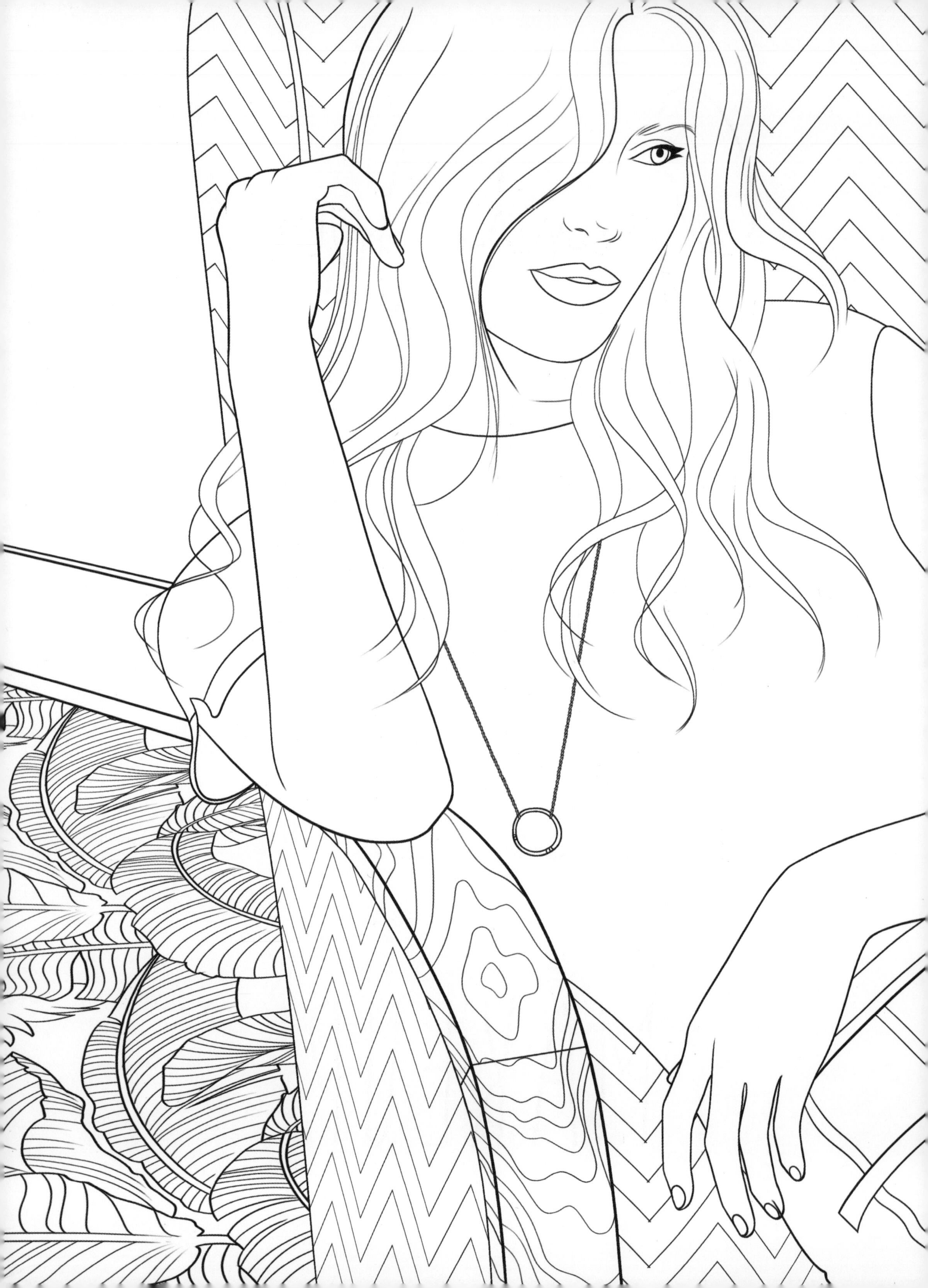

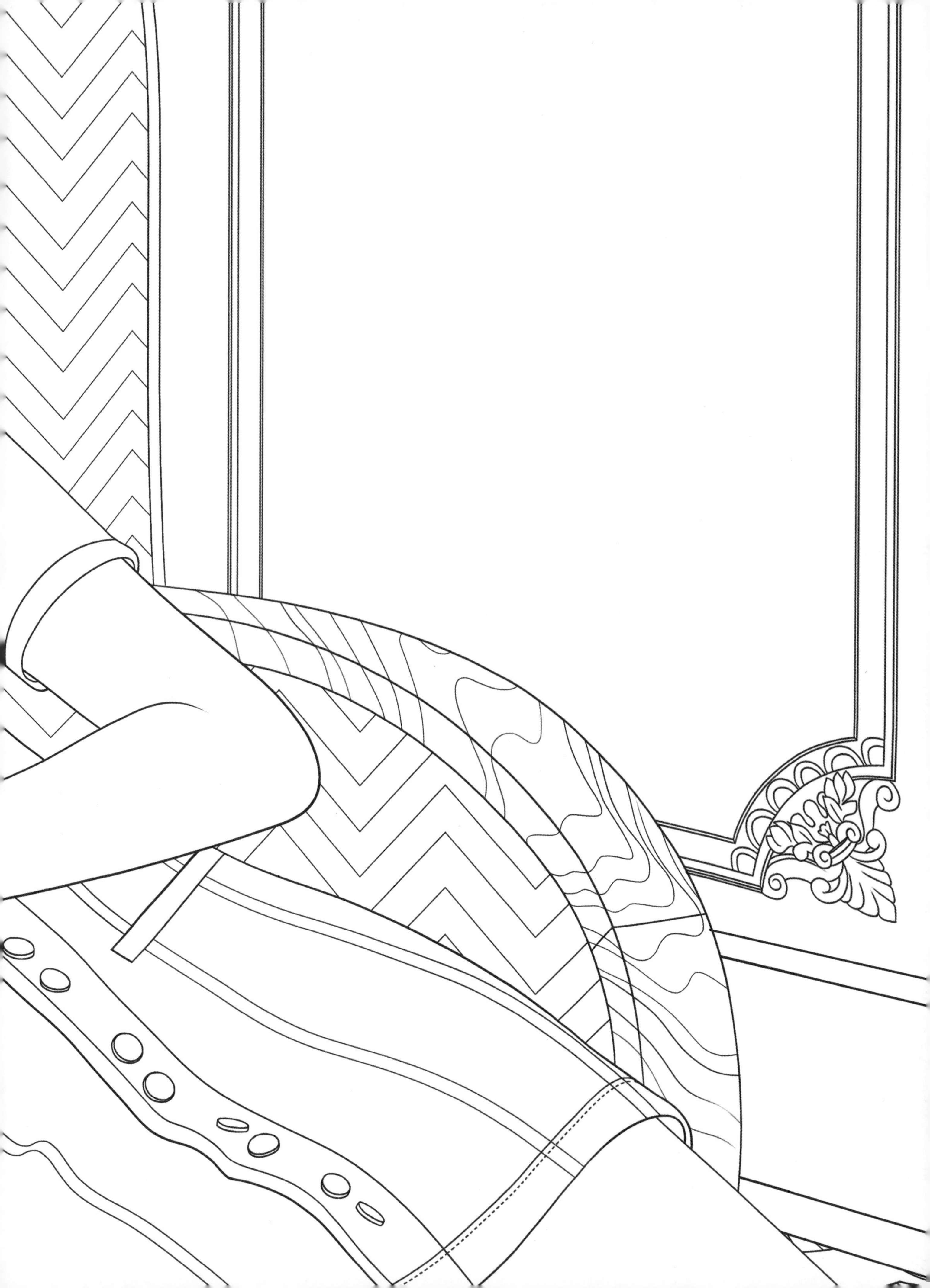

DESIGN
YOUR
FAVORITE
PRINTS

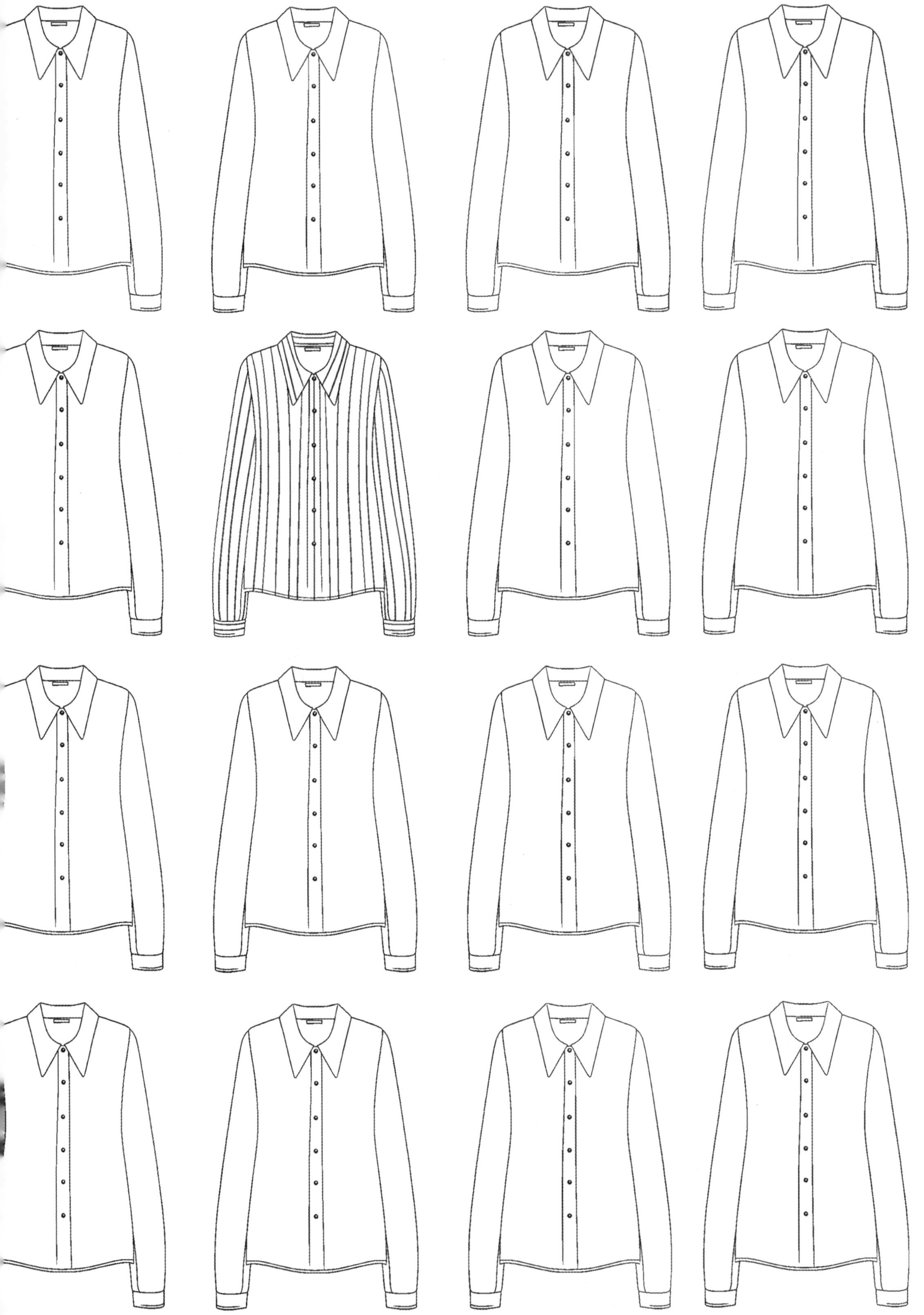

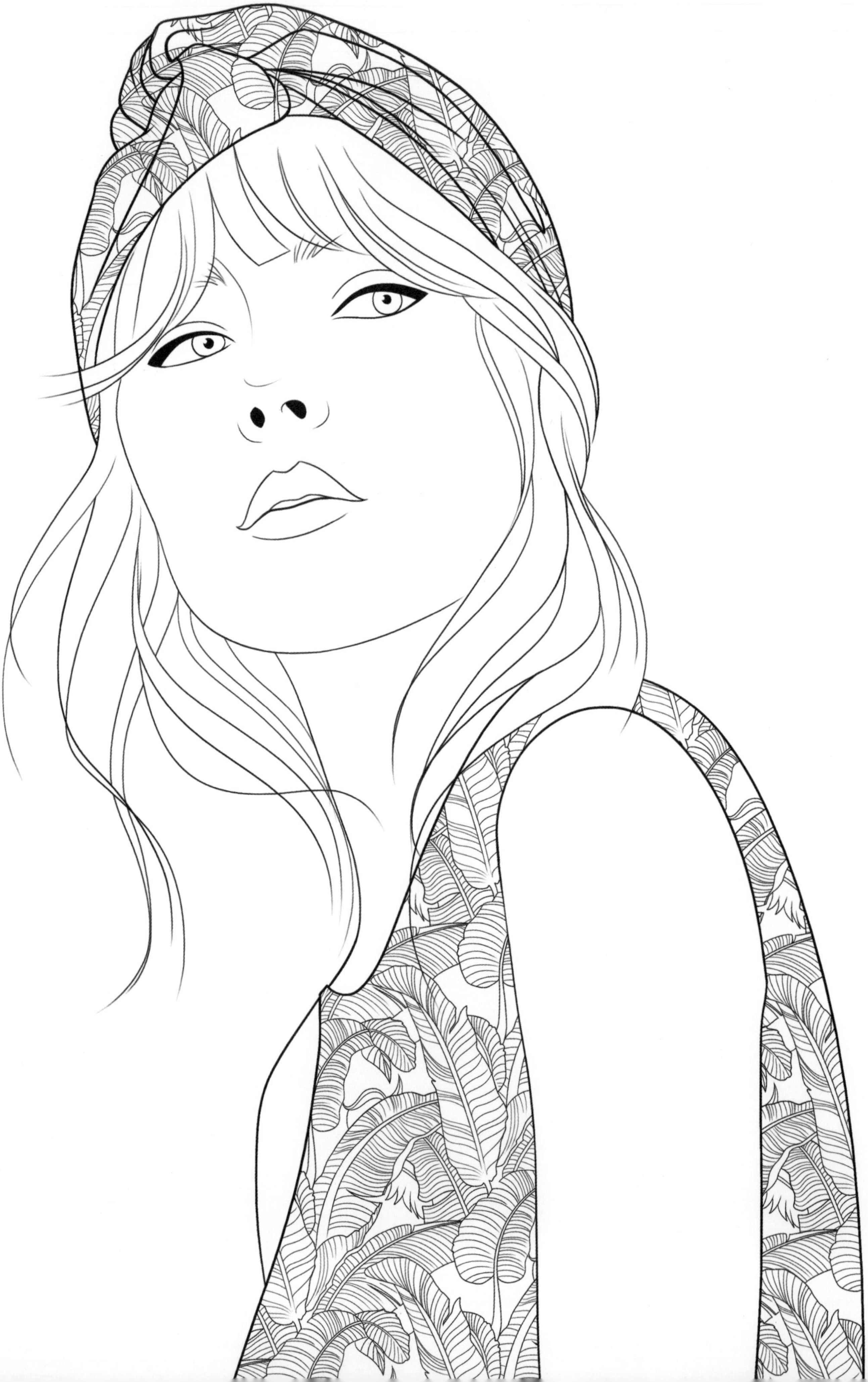

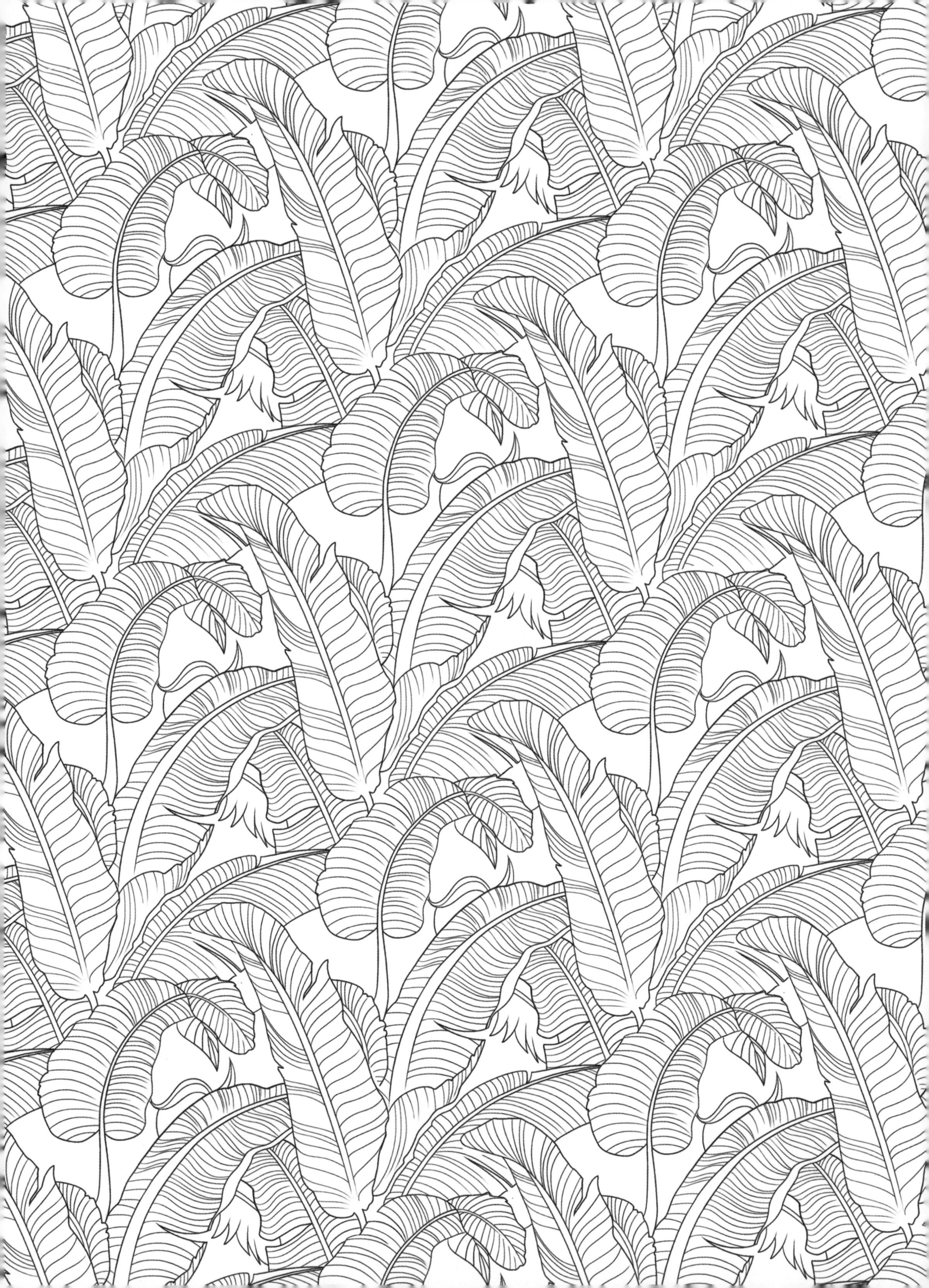

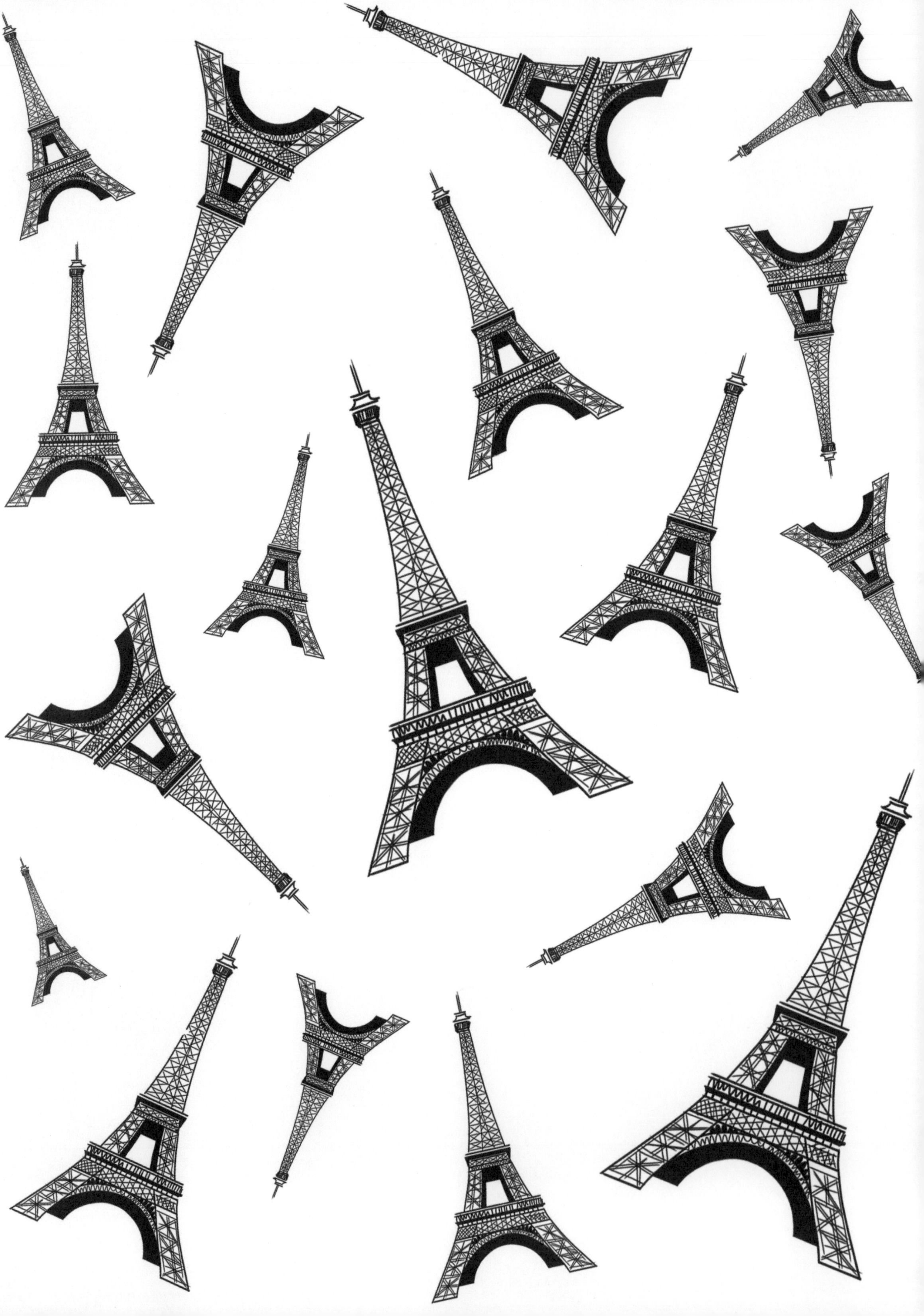

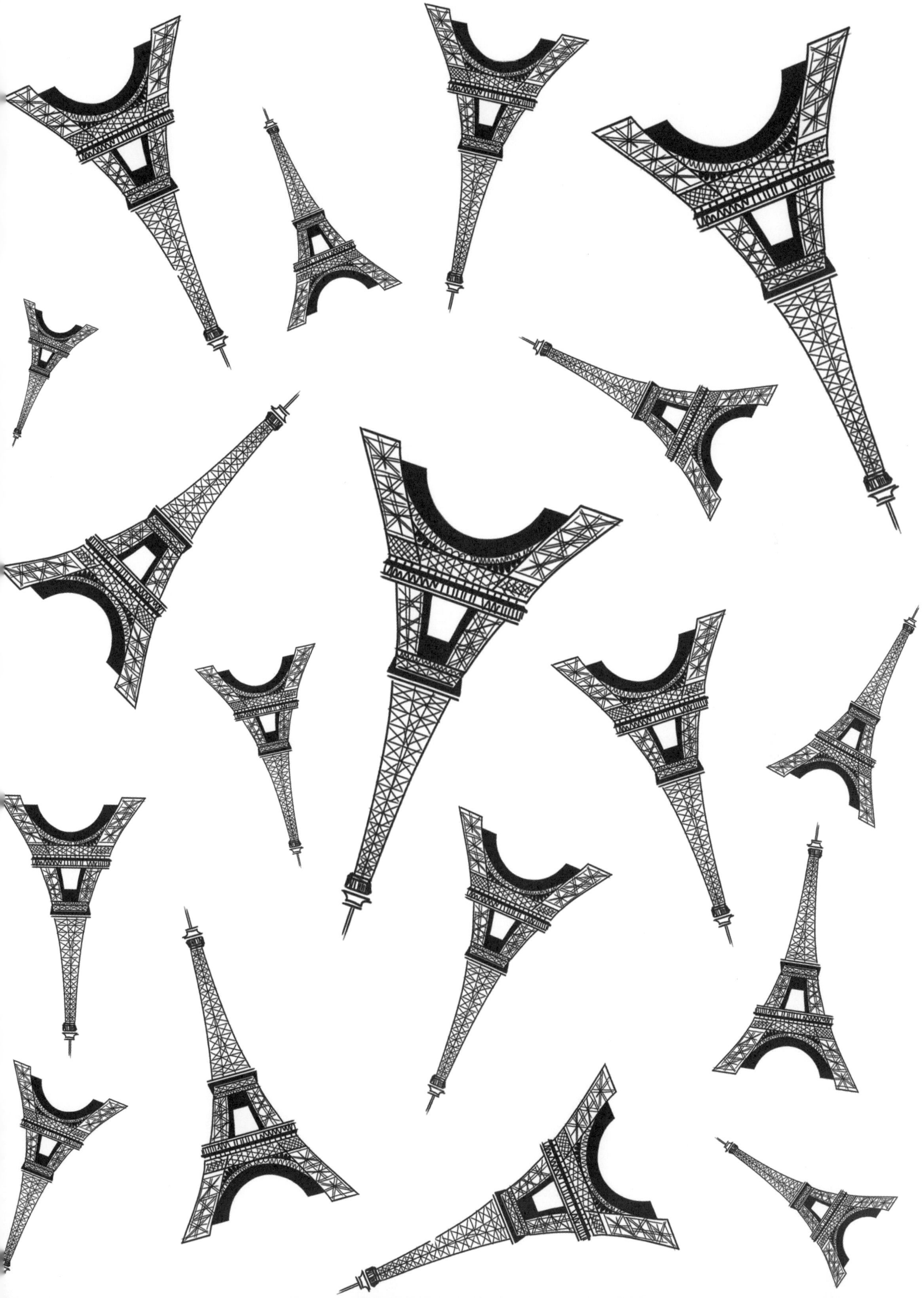

2ᵐᵉ ARRᵗ

RUE VIVIENNE

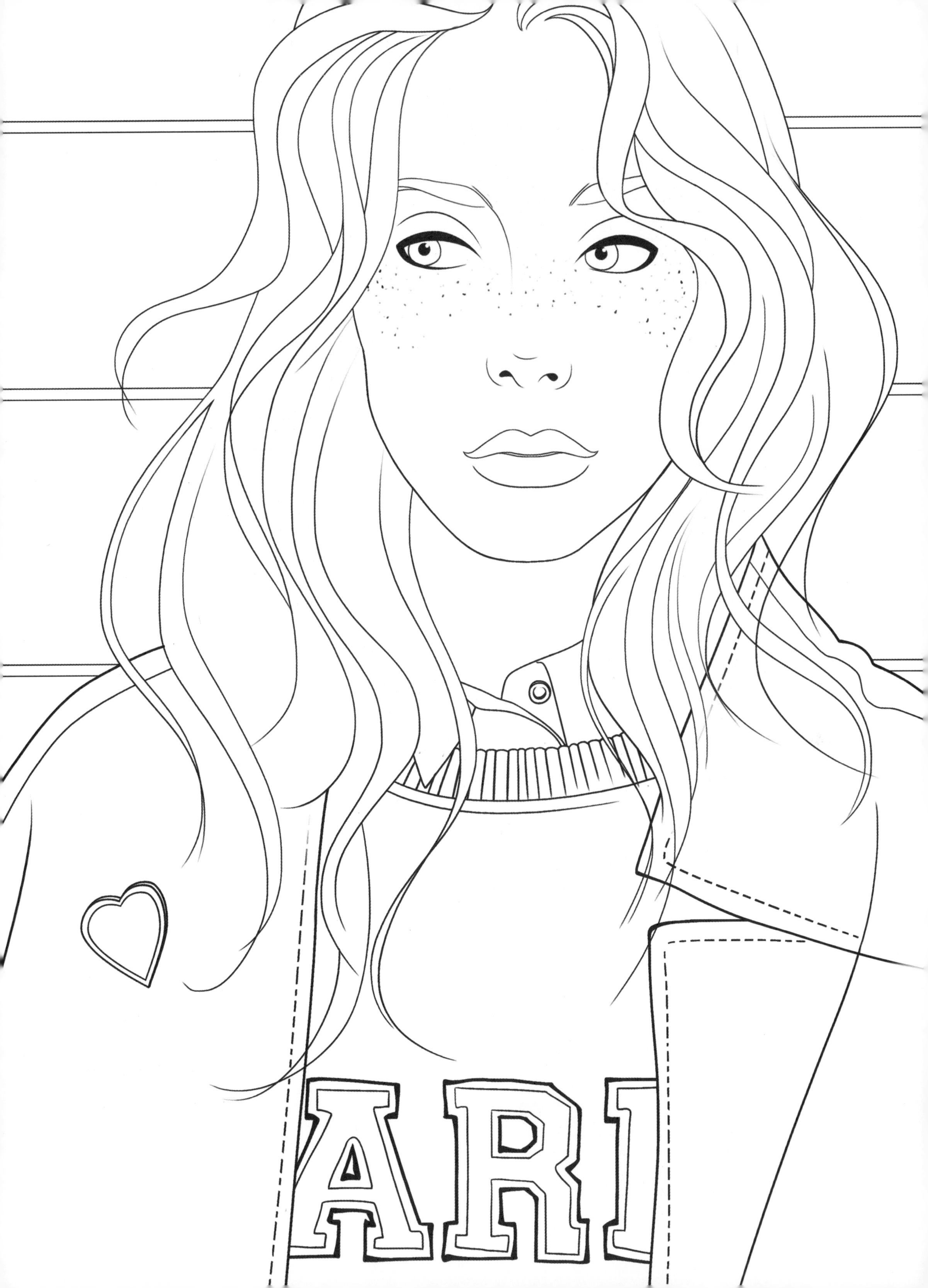
ARI

ISABELLE
Adjani

Jean Giraudoux
Ondine

classique

LE PULL MARINE

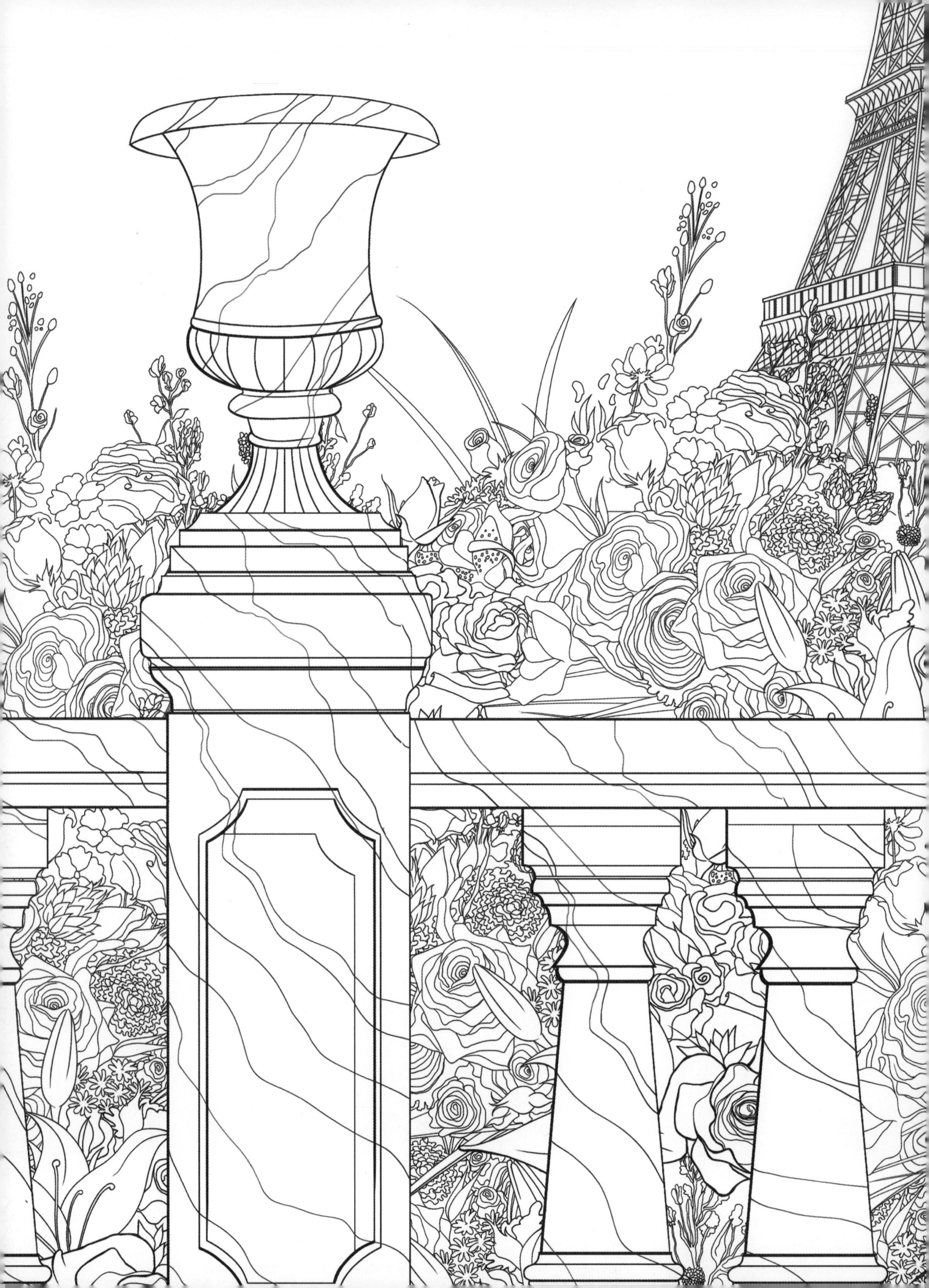

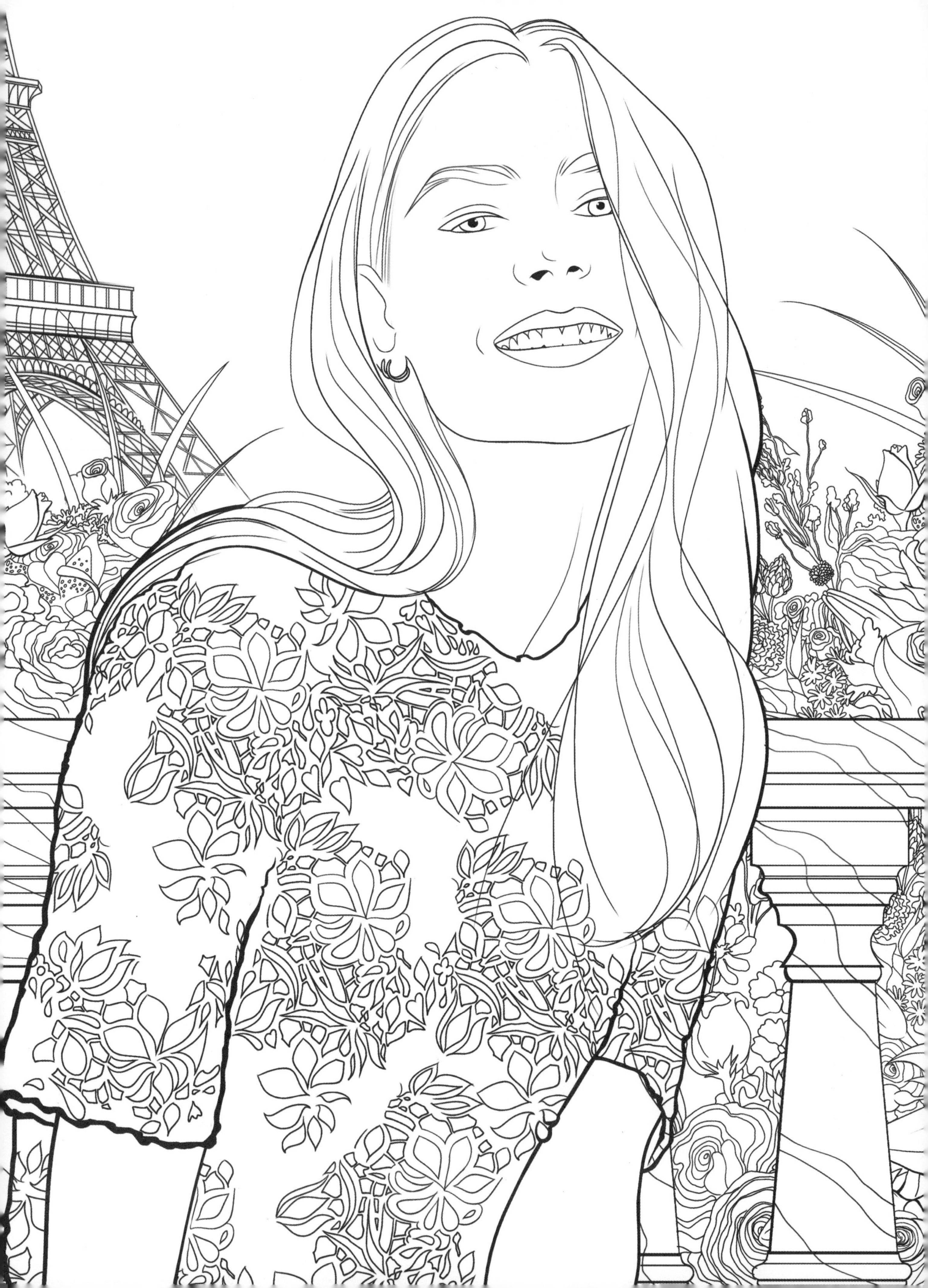

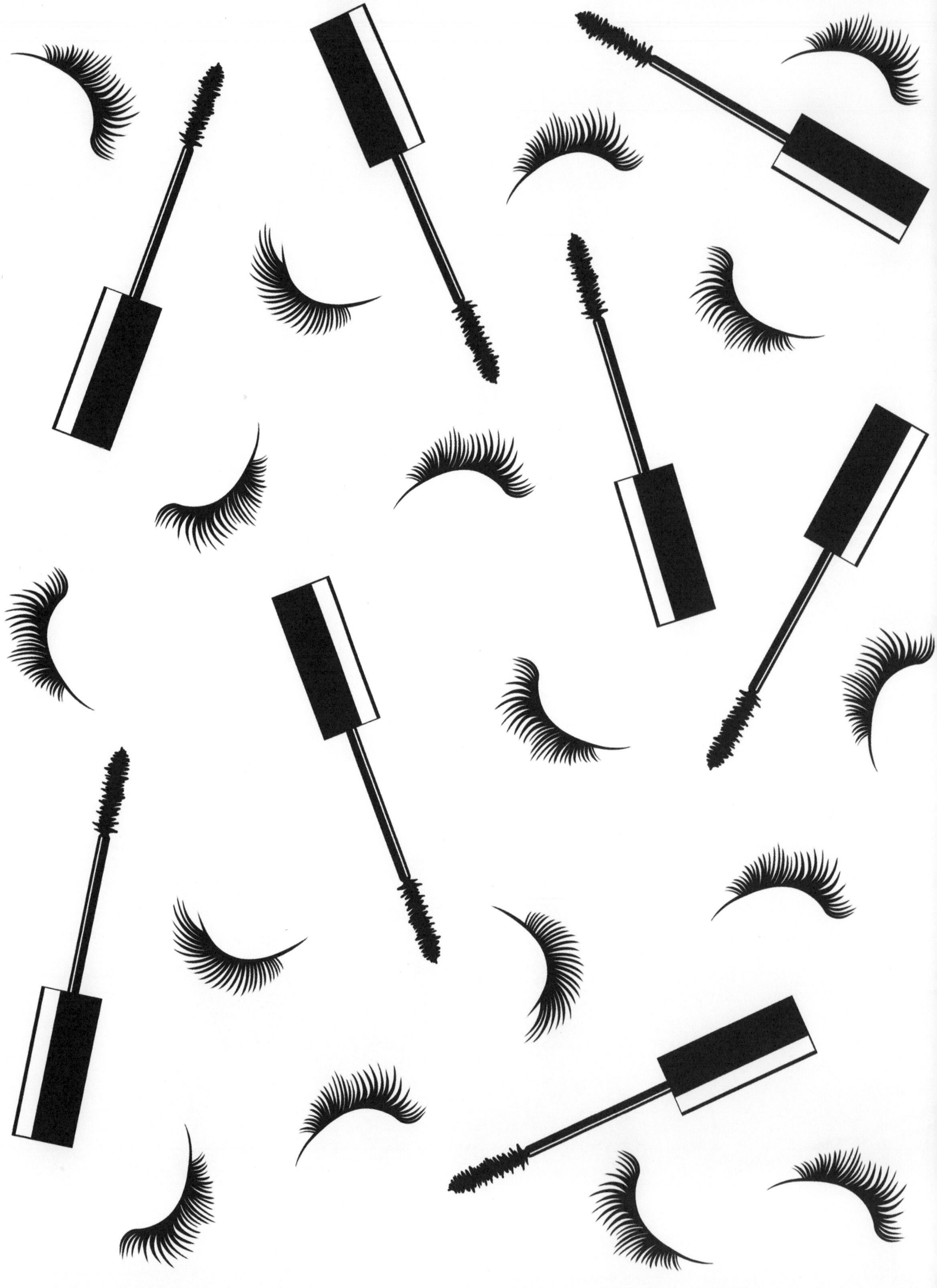

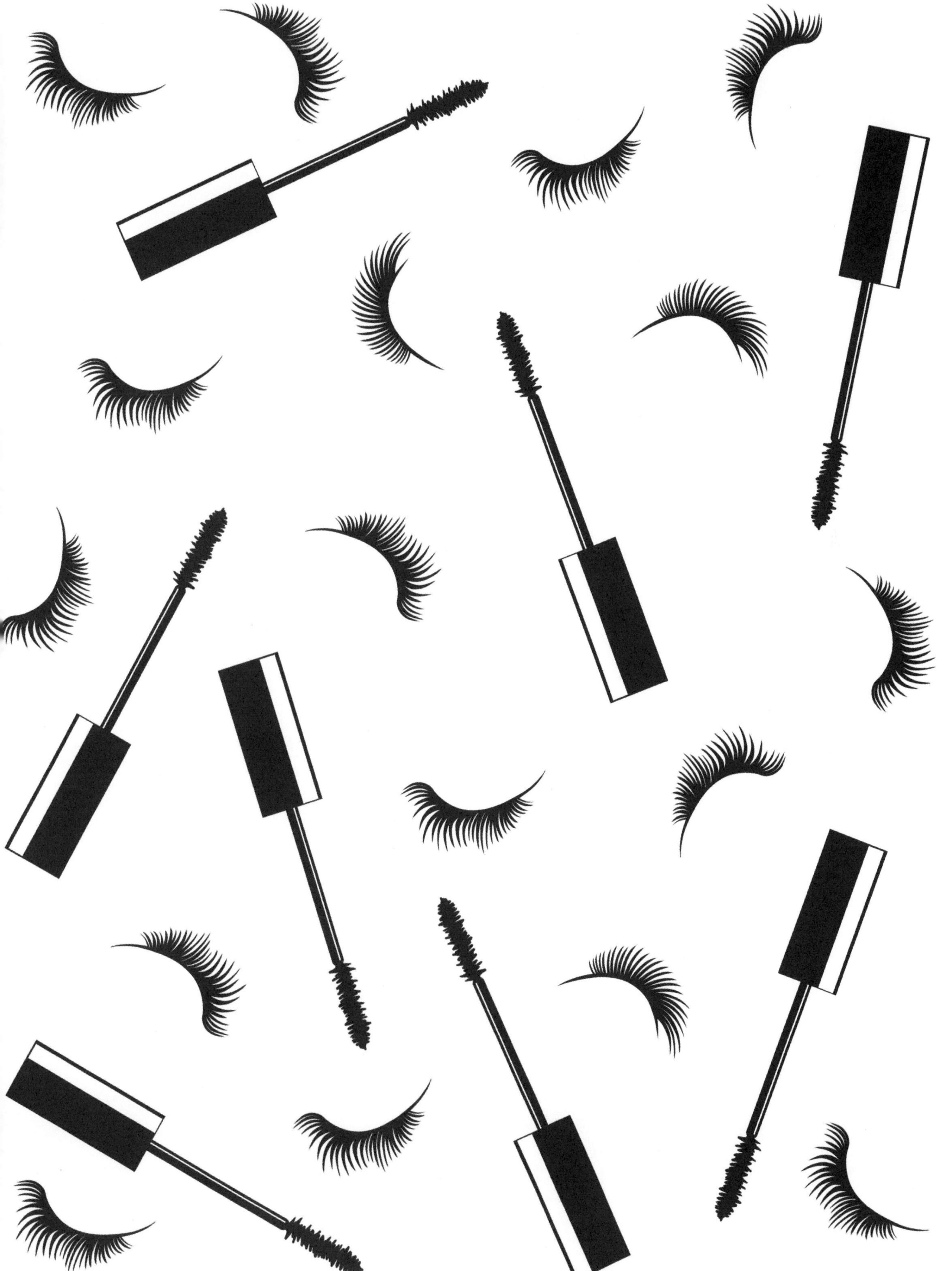

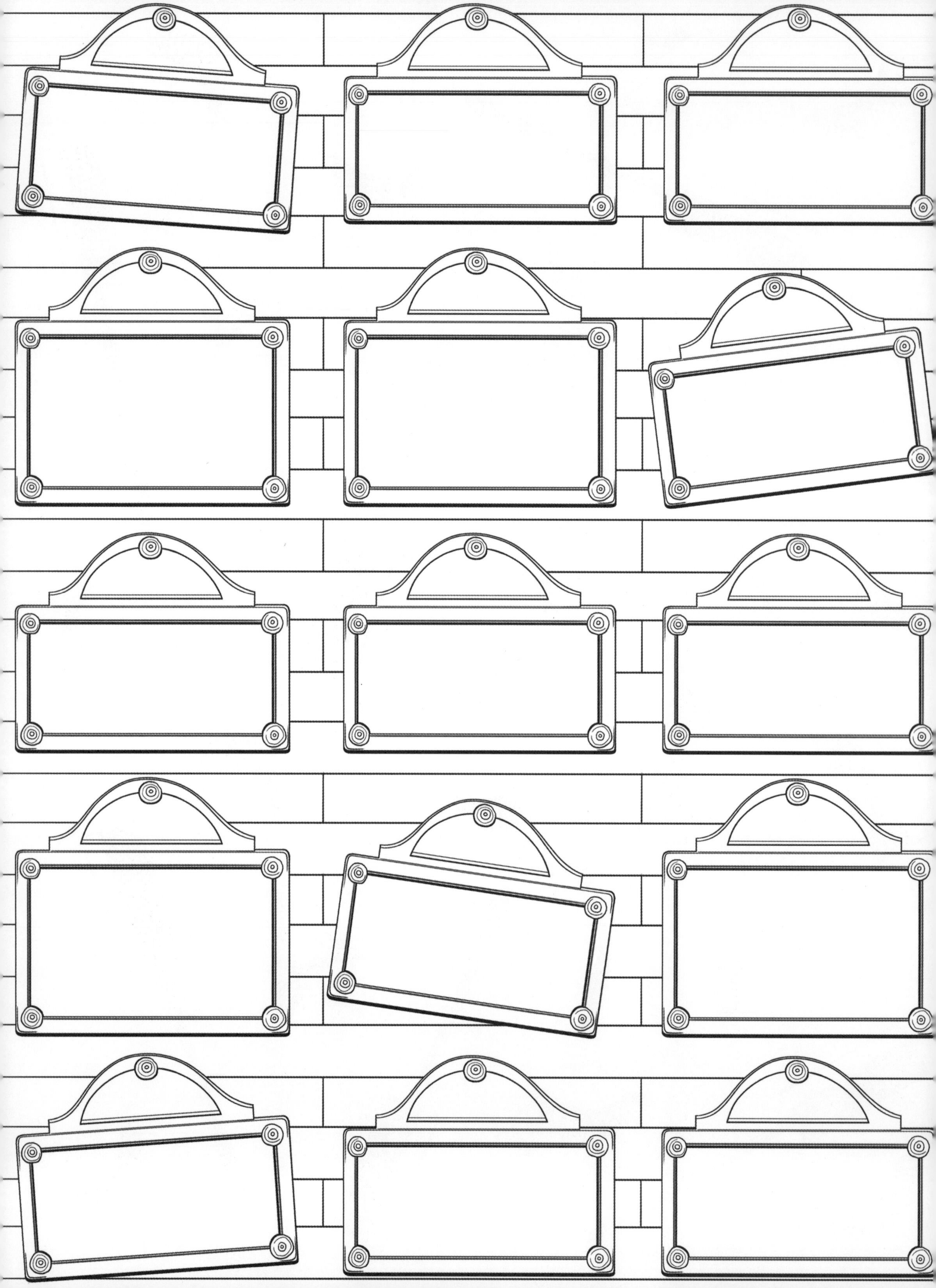

WHAT ARE
YOUR FAVORITE
PARISIENNE
STREETS?

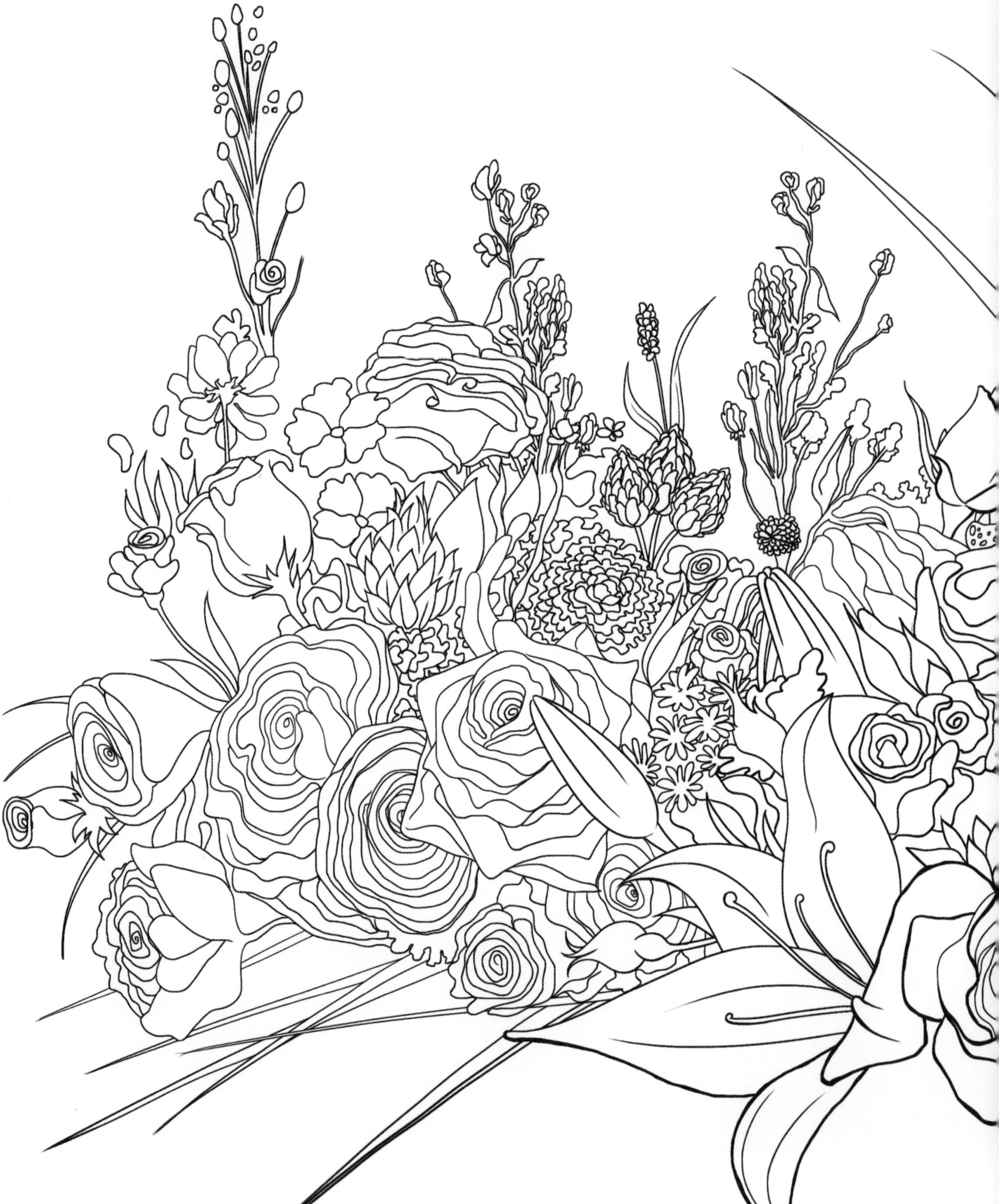

CUSTOMIZE YOUR BAG WITH THE COLORS OF SPRING

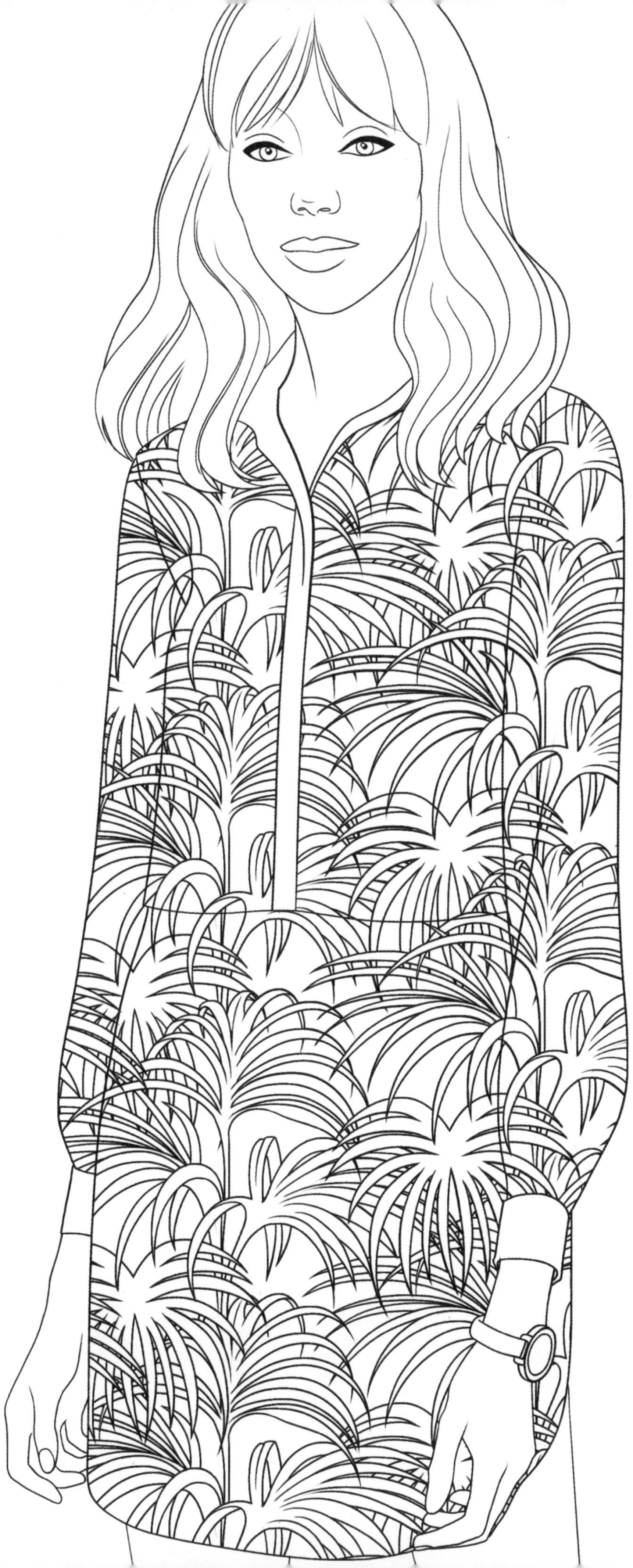

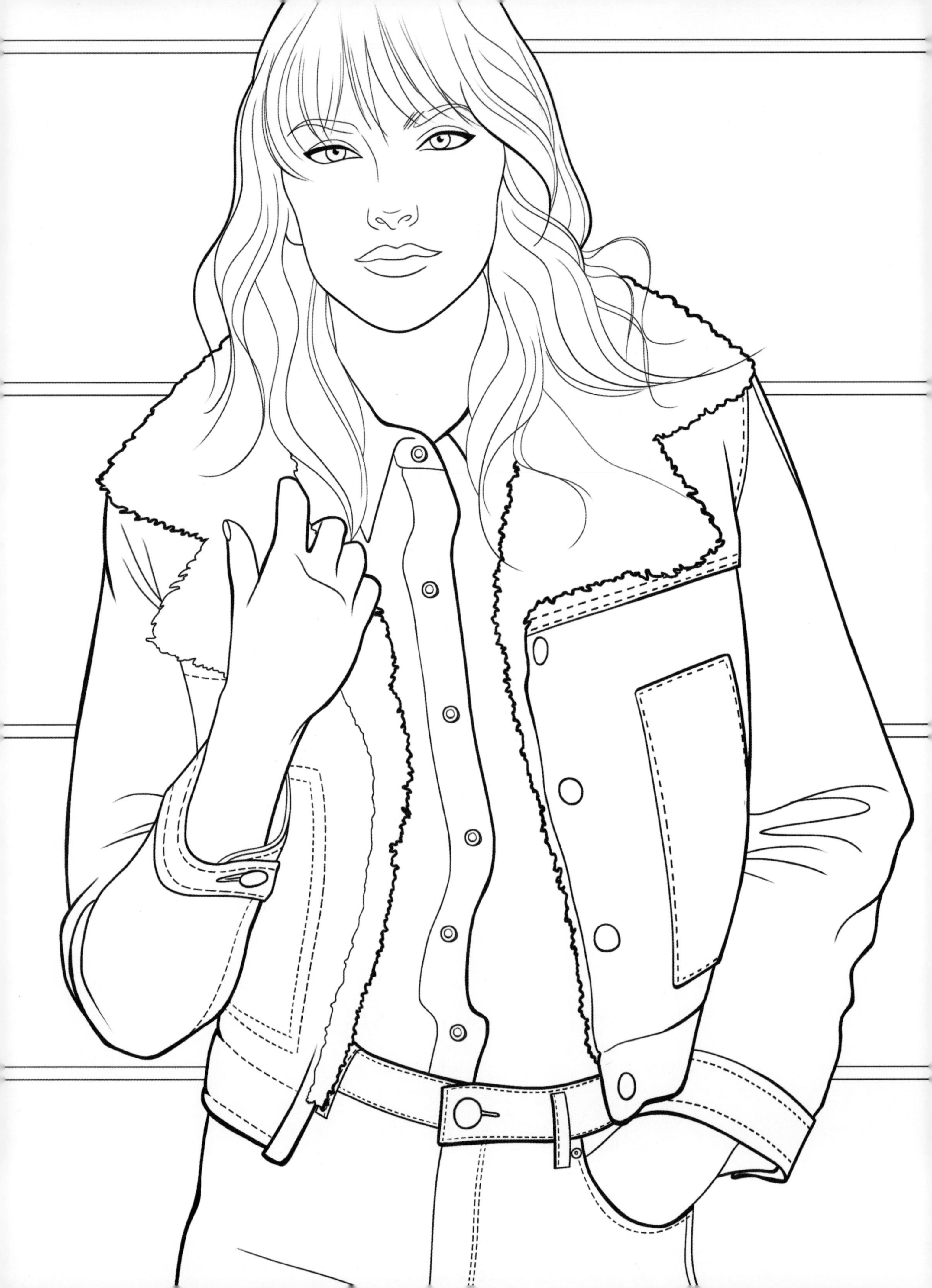

2ᵐᵉ . ARRᵗ

RUE MONTMARTRE

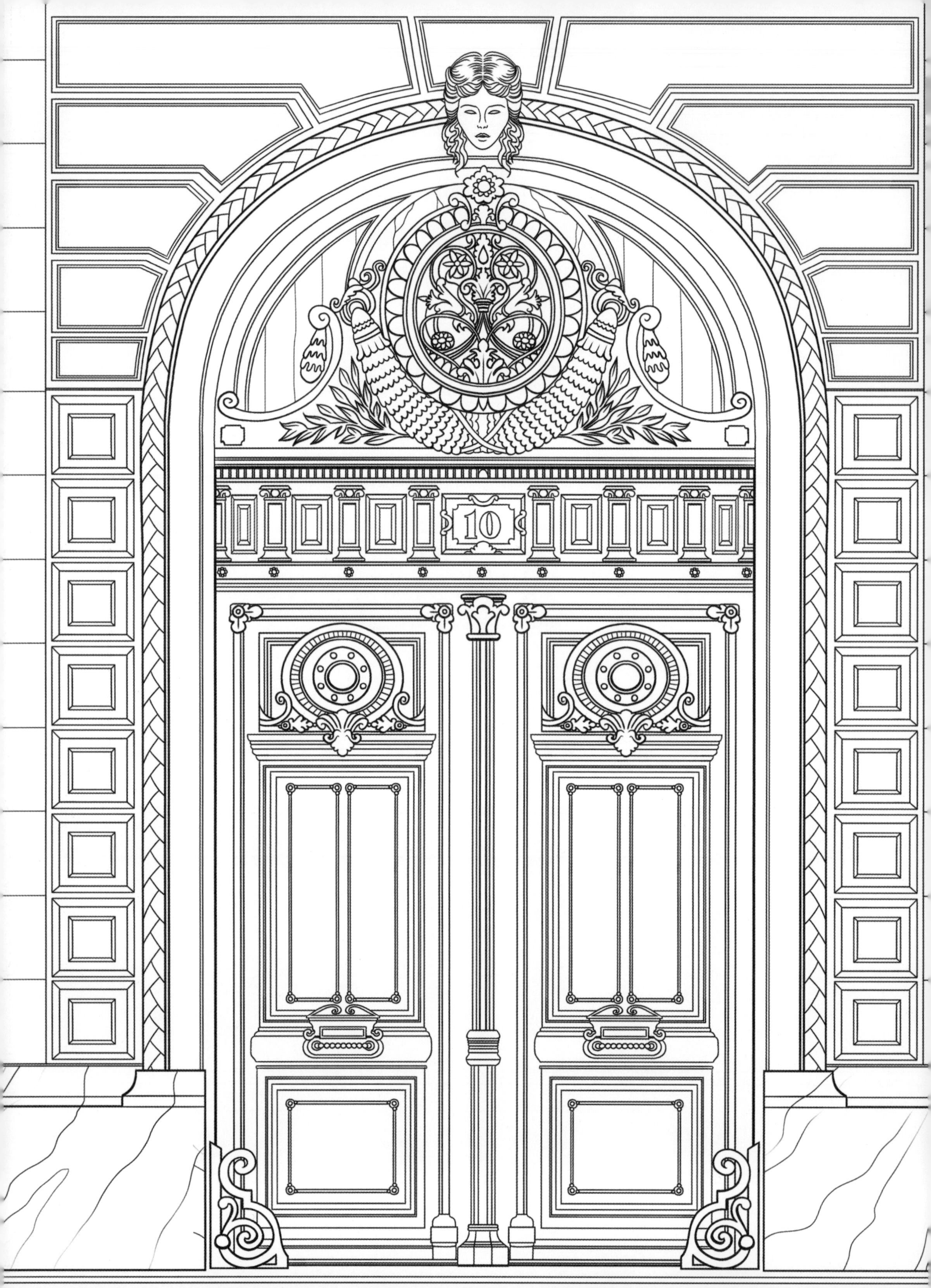
10

C'EST L'ÉTÉ...

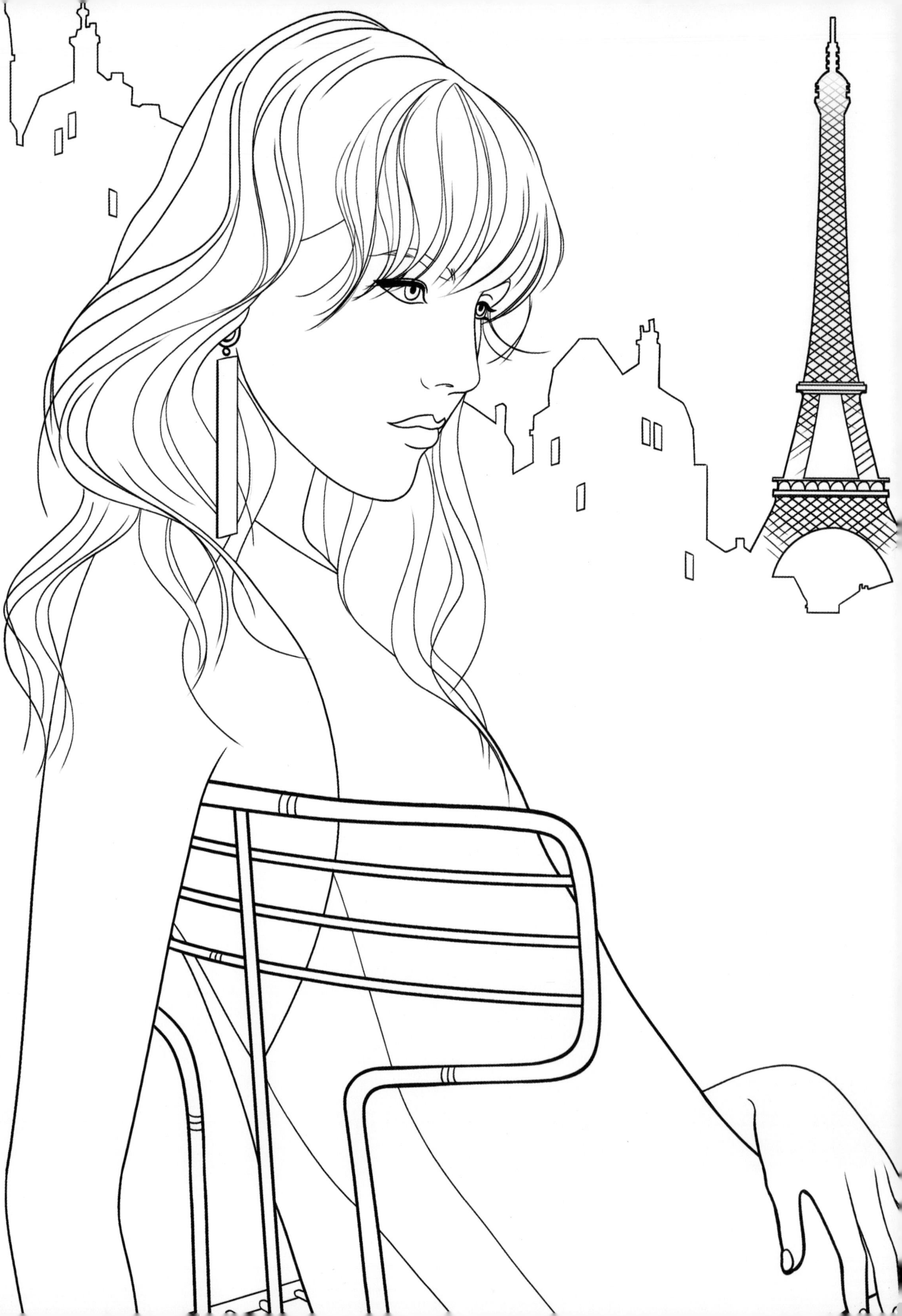

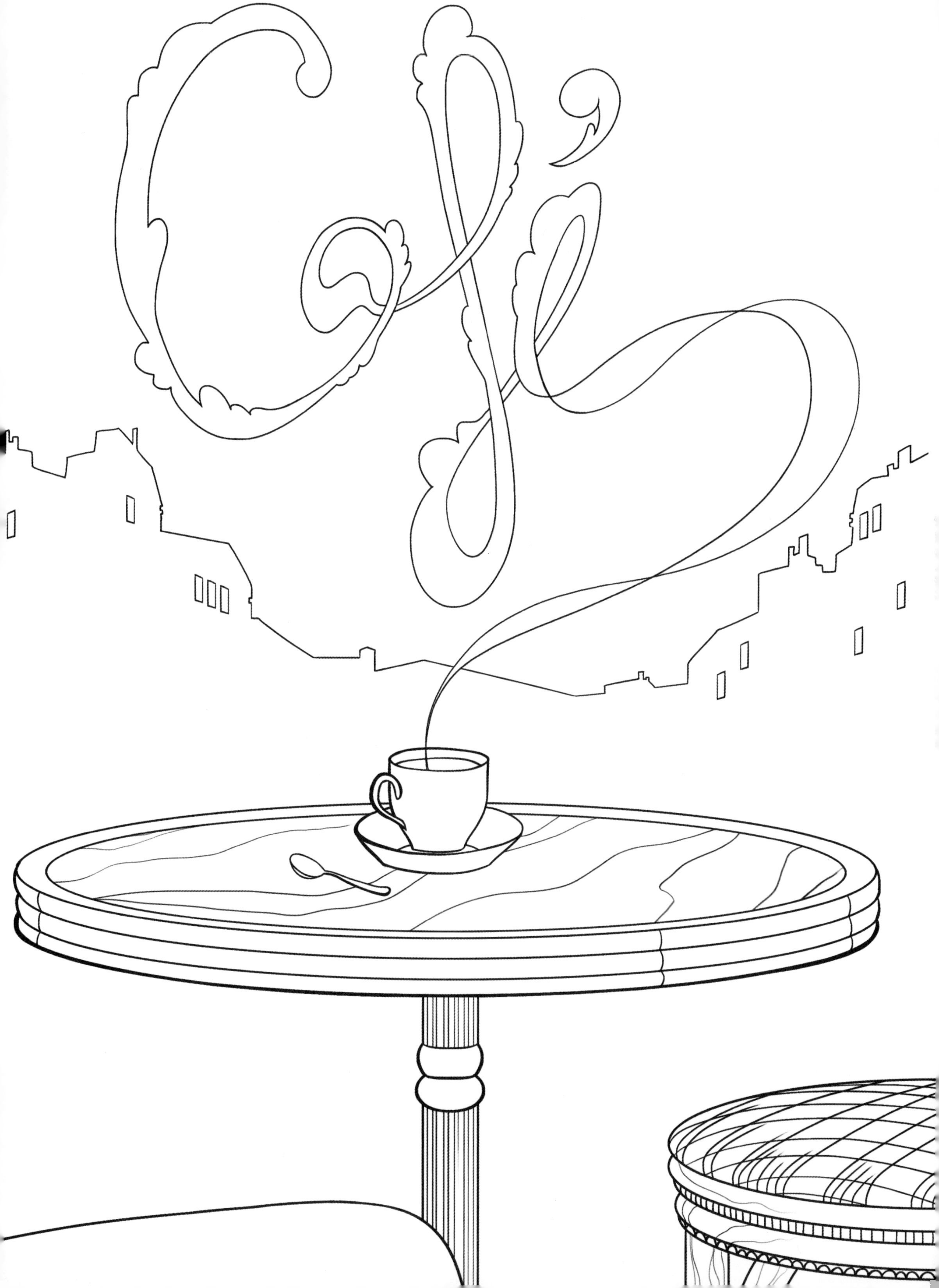
Café

FRANÇOISE
Hardy

françoise

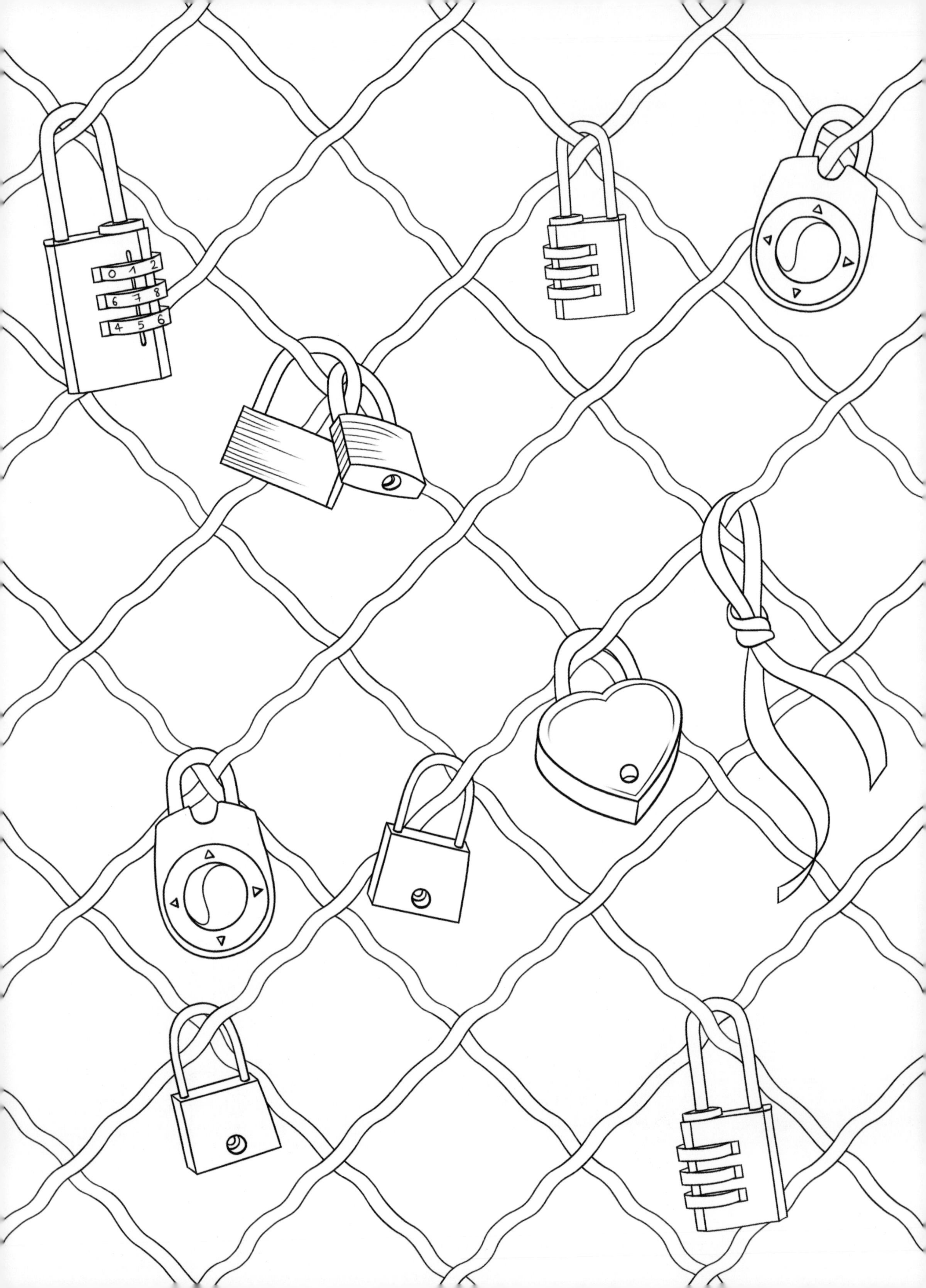
0 1 2
6 7 8
4 5 6

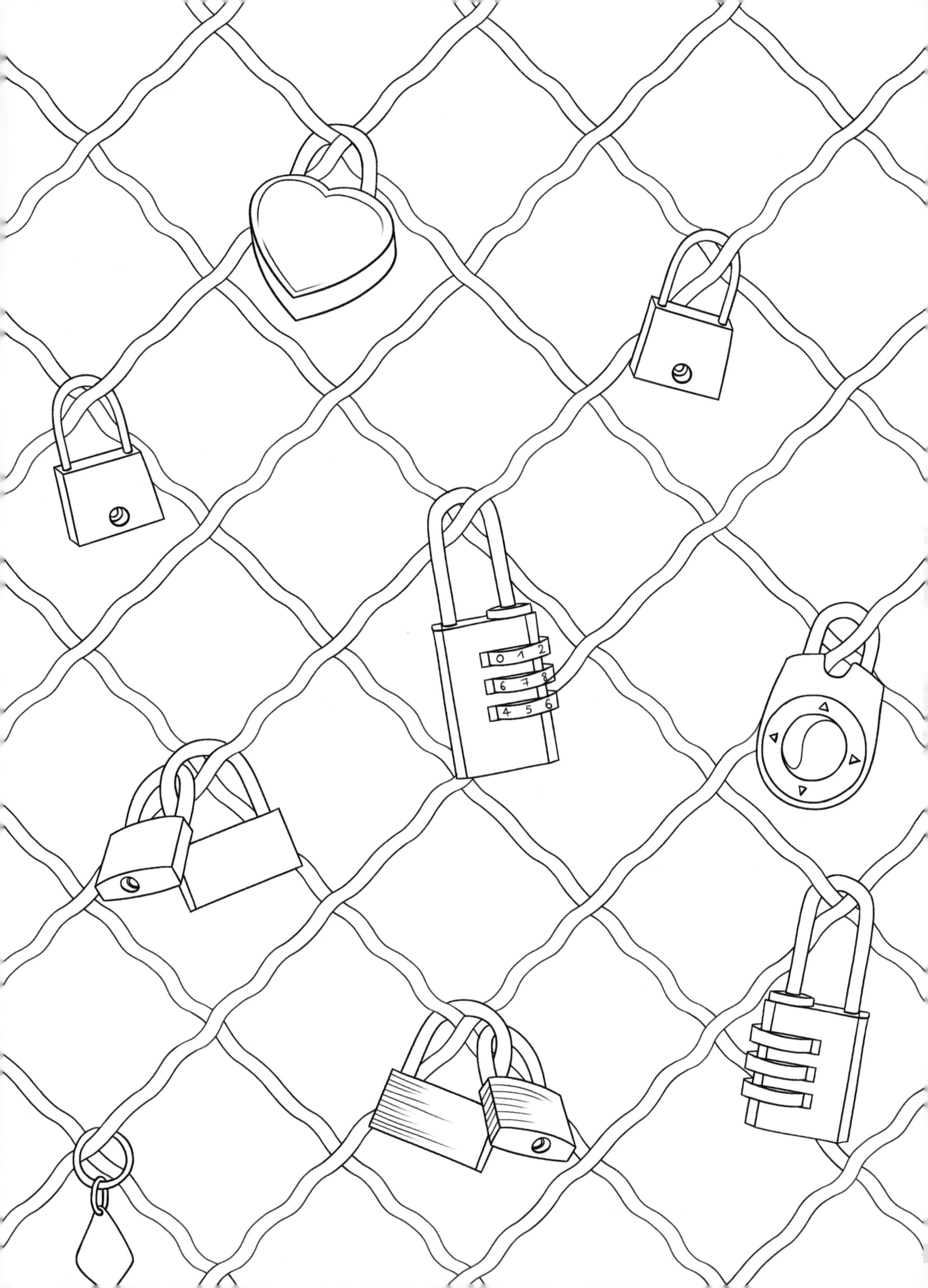
0 1 2
6 7 8
4 5 6

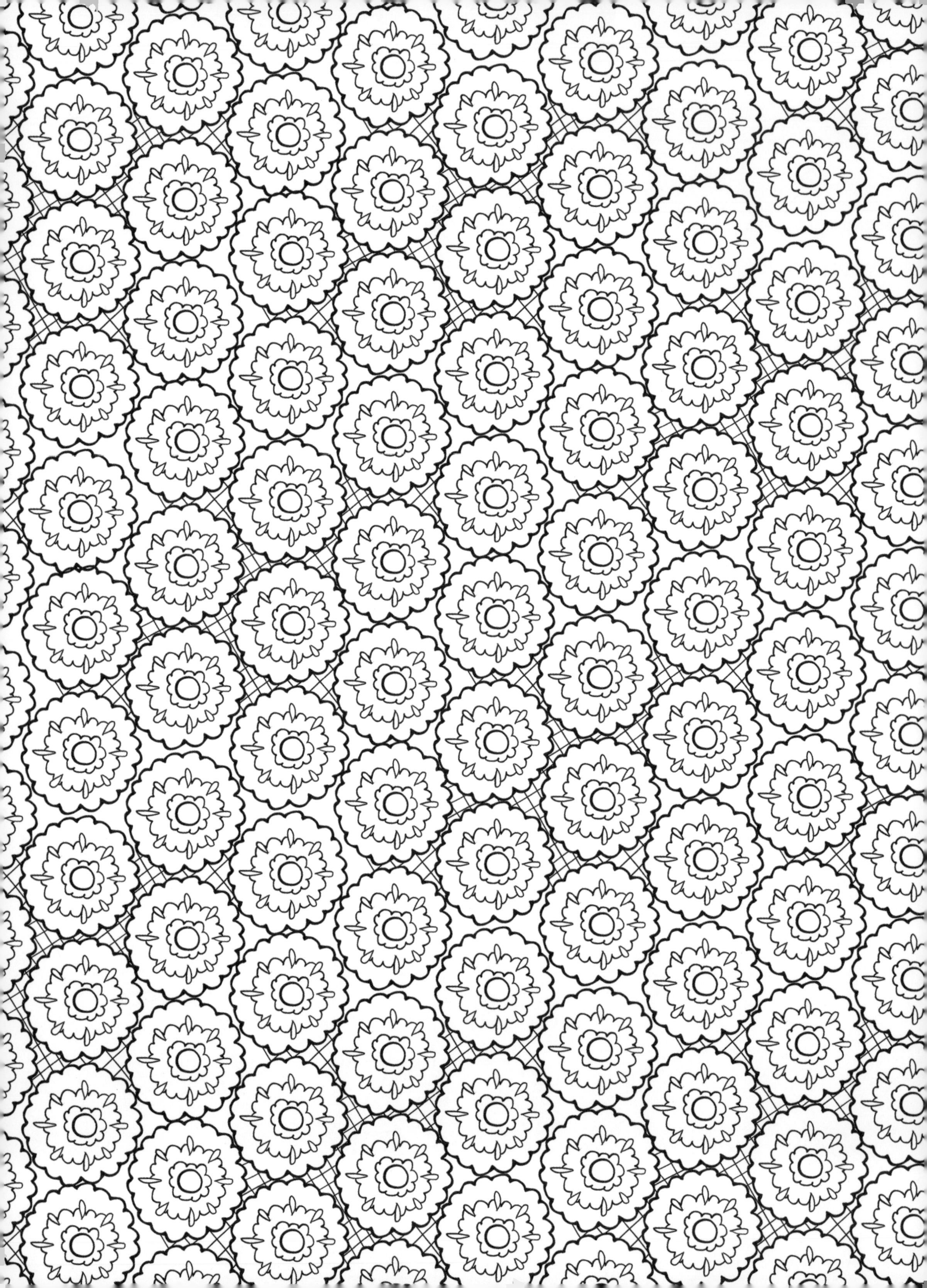

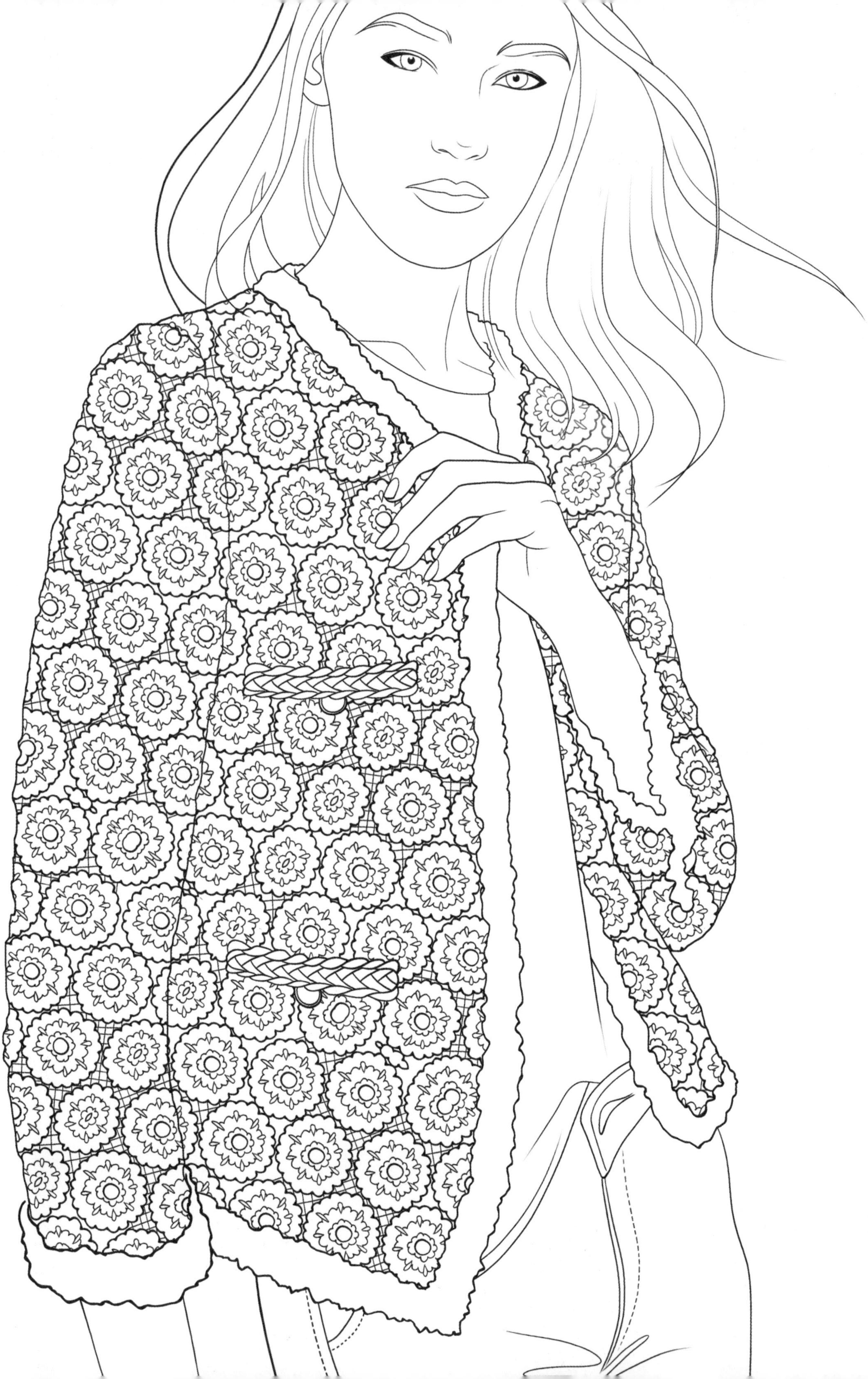

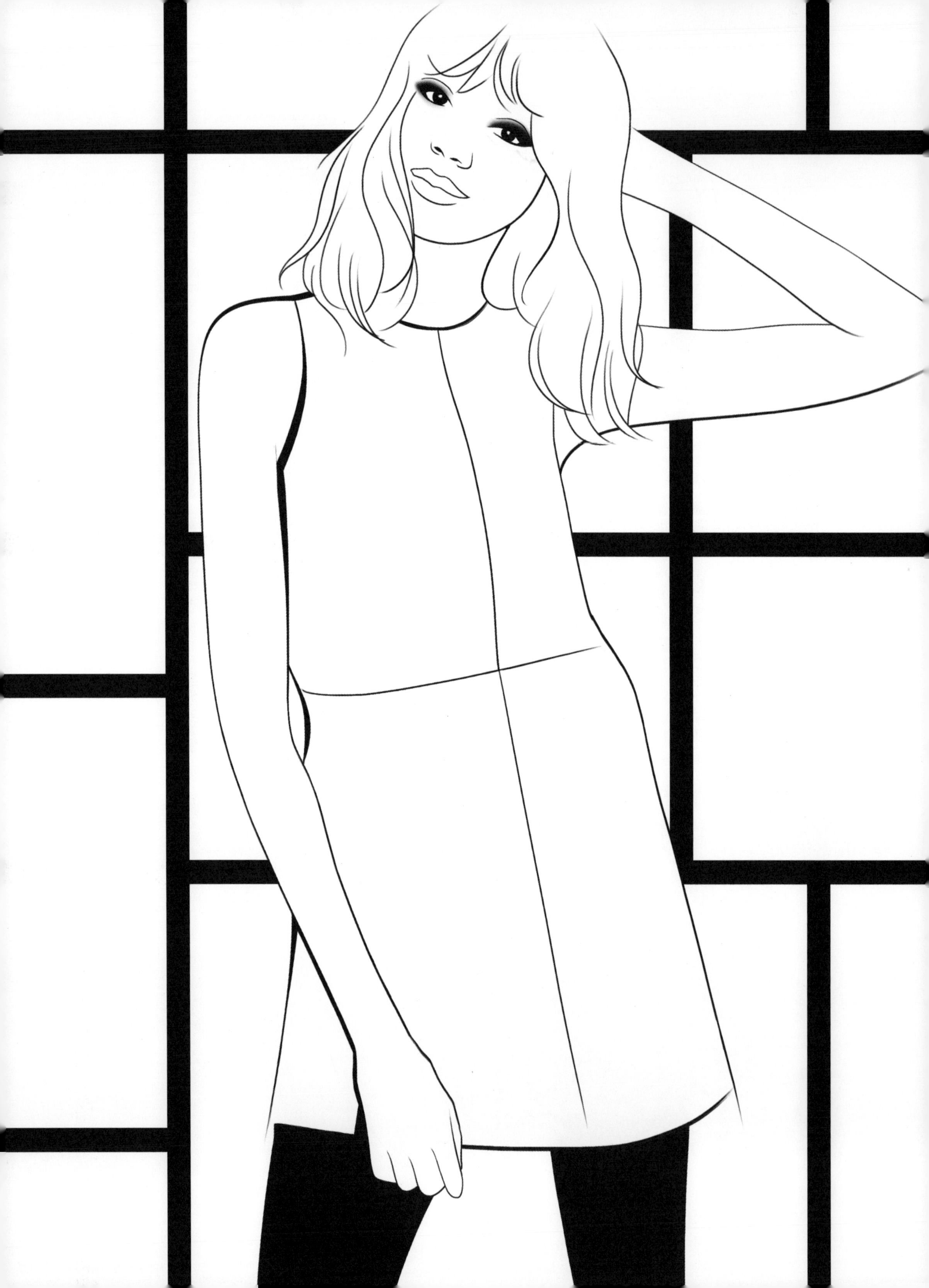

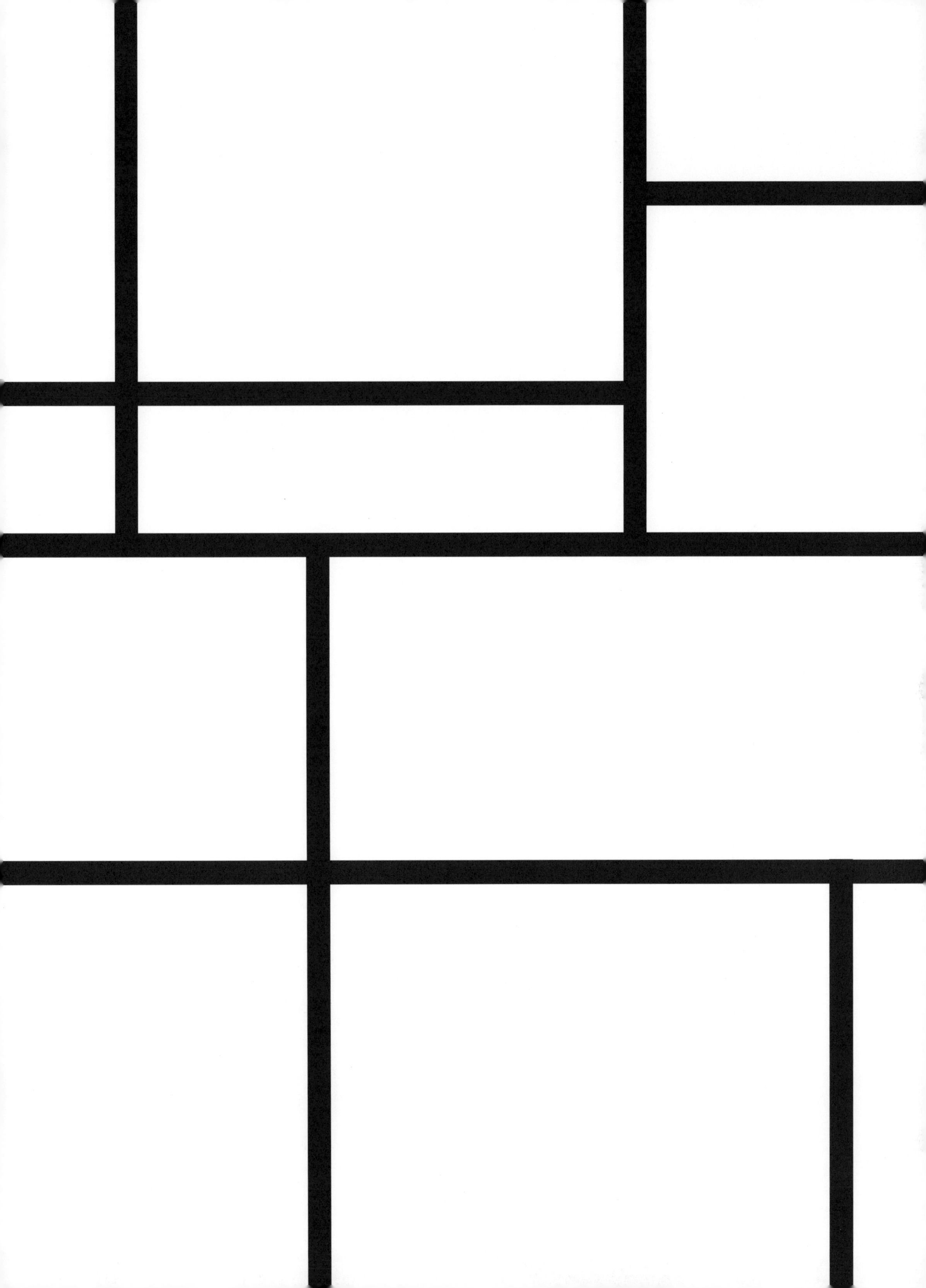

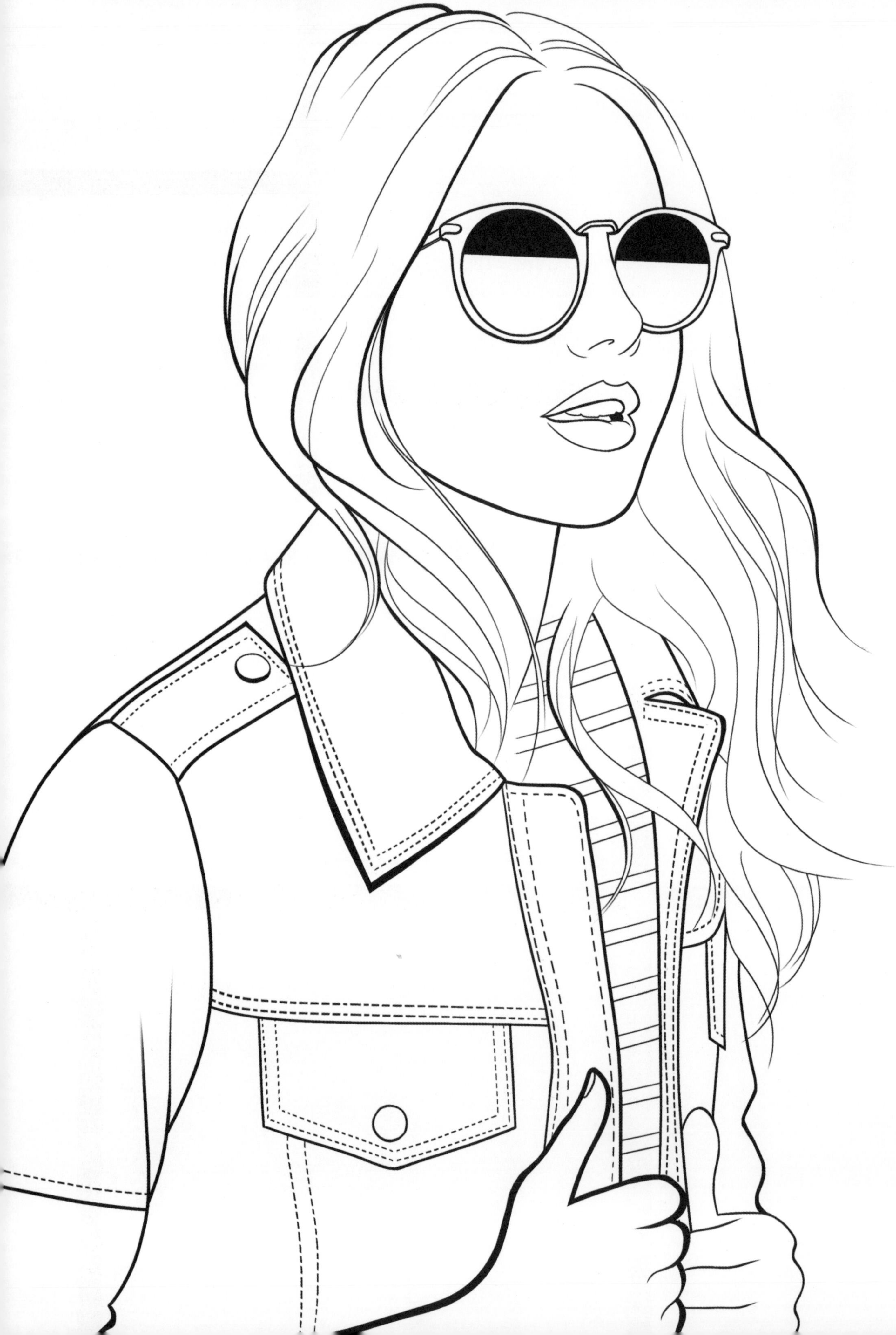

COLOR YOUR OUTLOOK!

LES TRÉSORS DU LOUVRE

Chloé

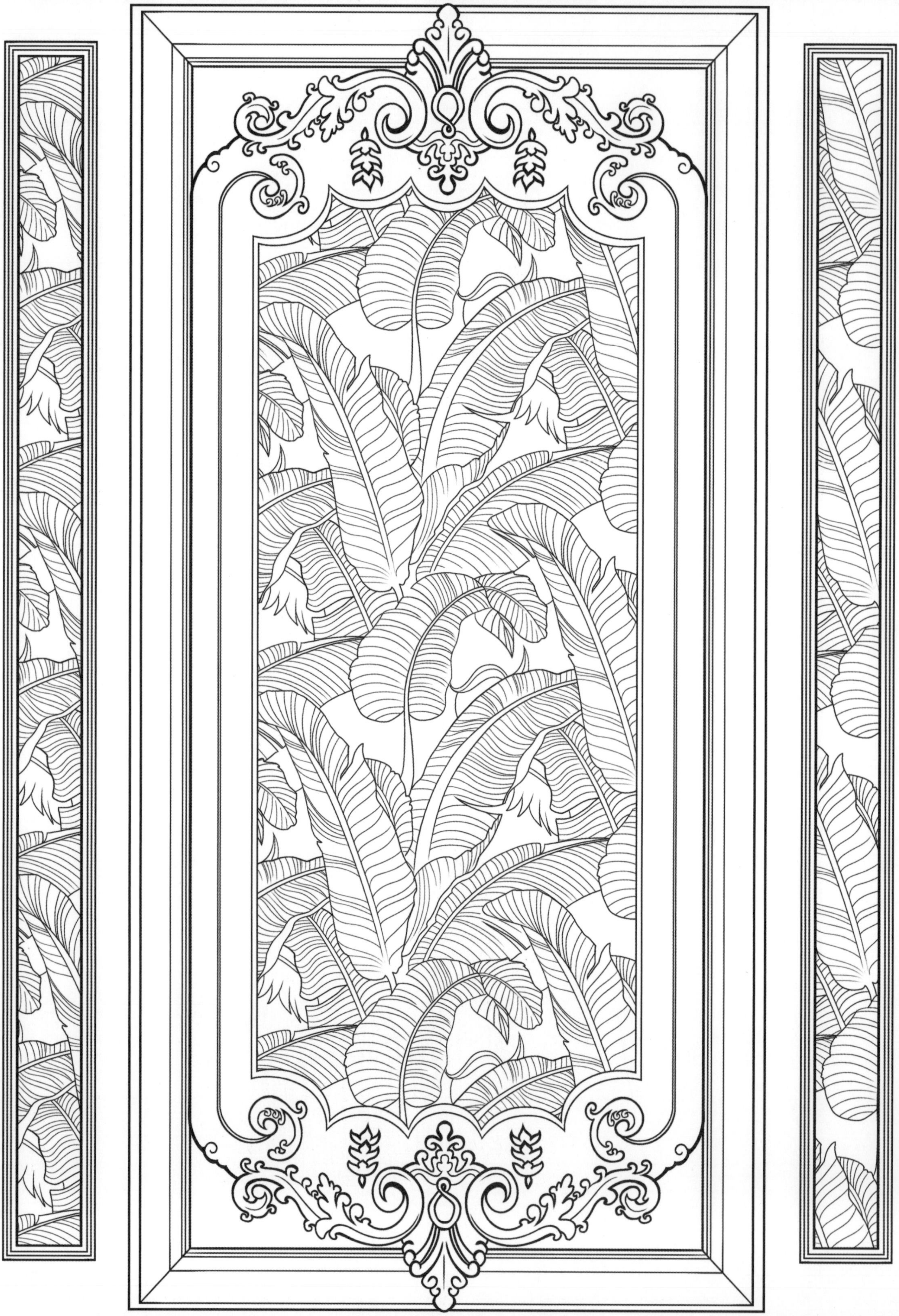

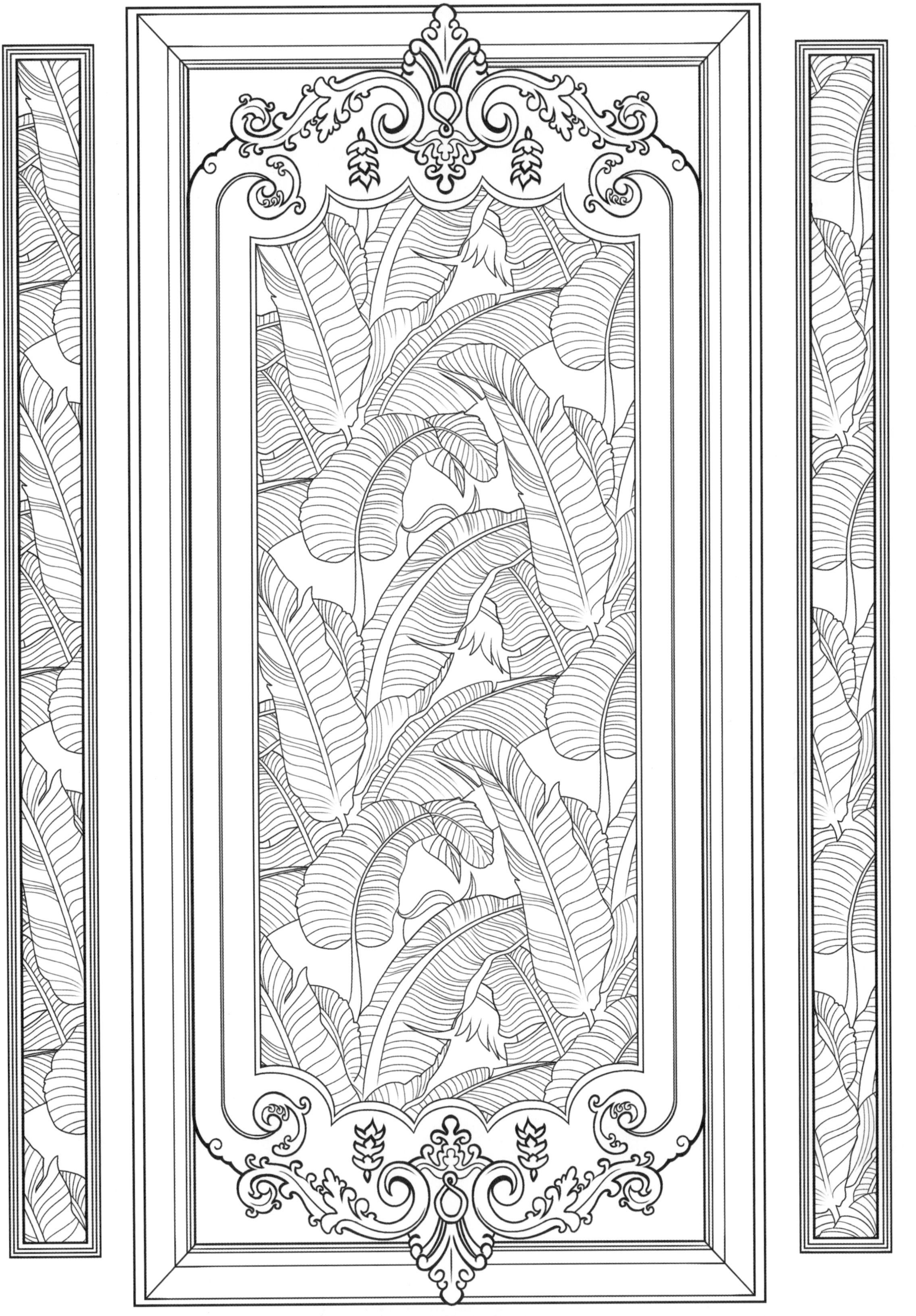

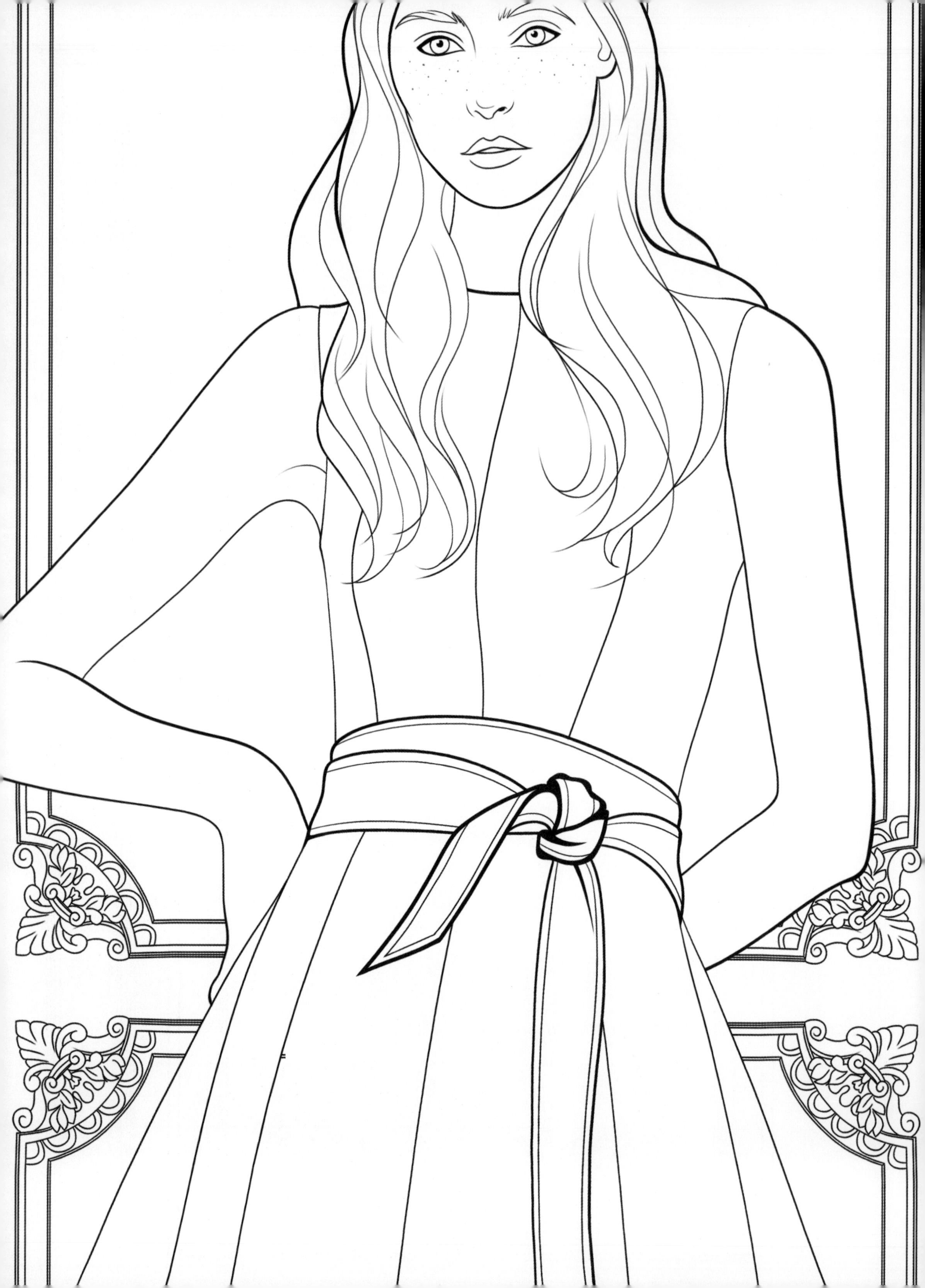

La petite robe noire

TRANSFORM YOUR LITTLE BLACK DRESS

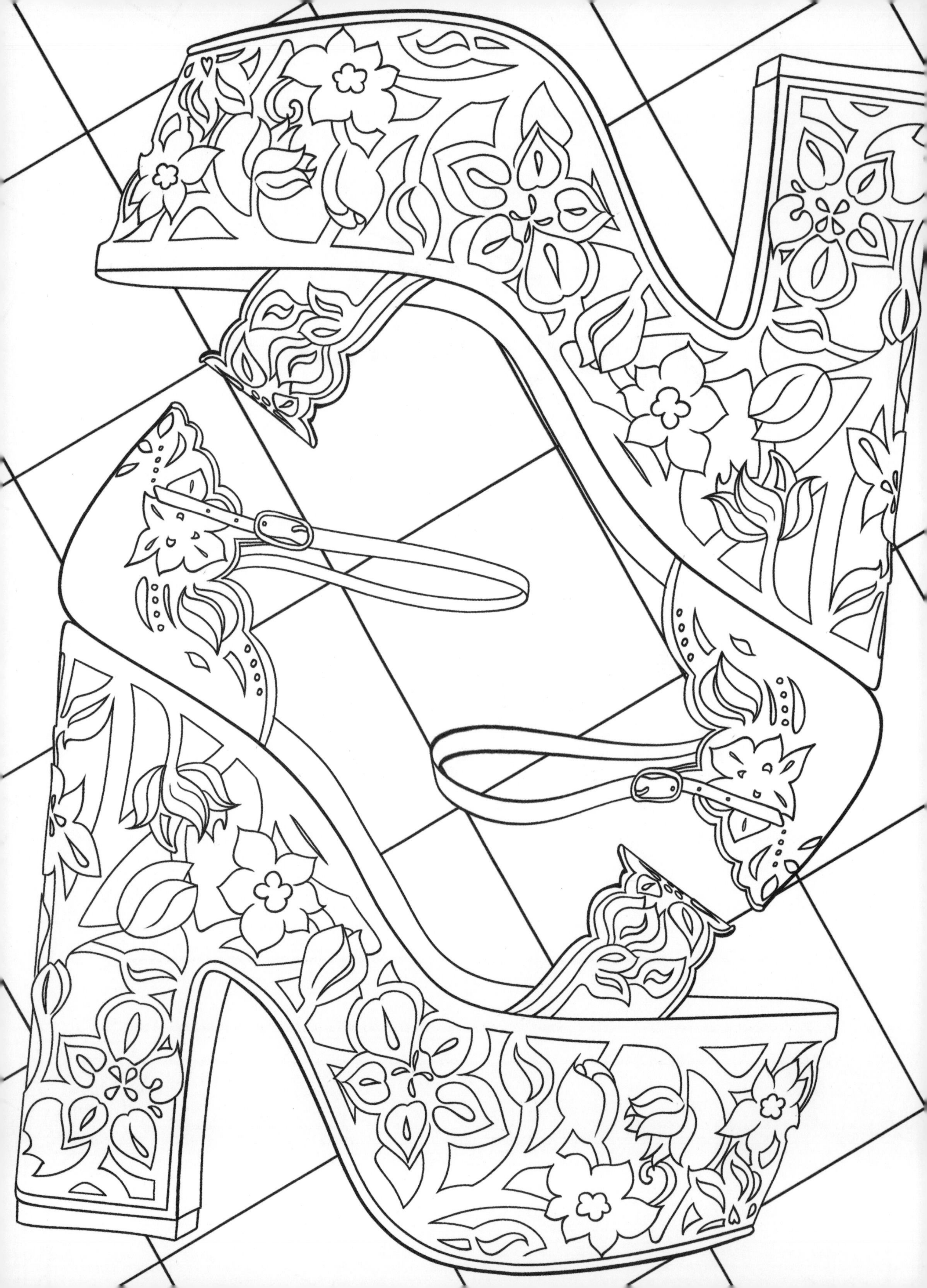

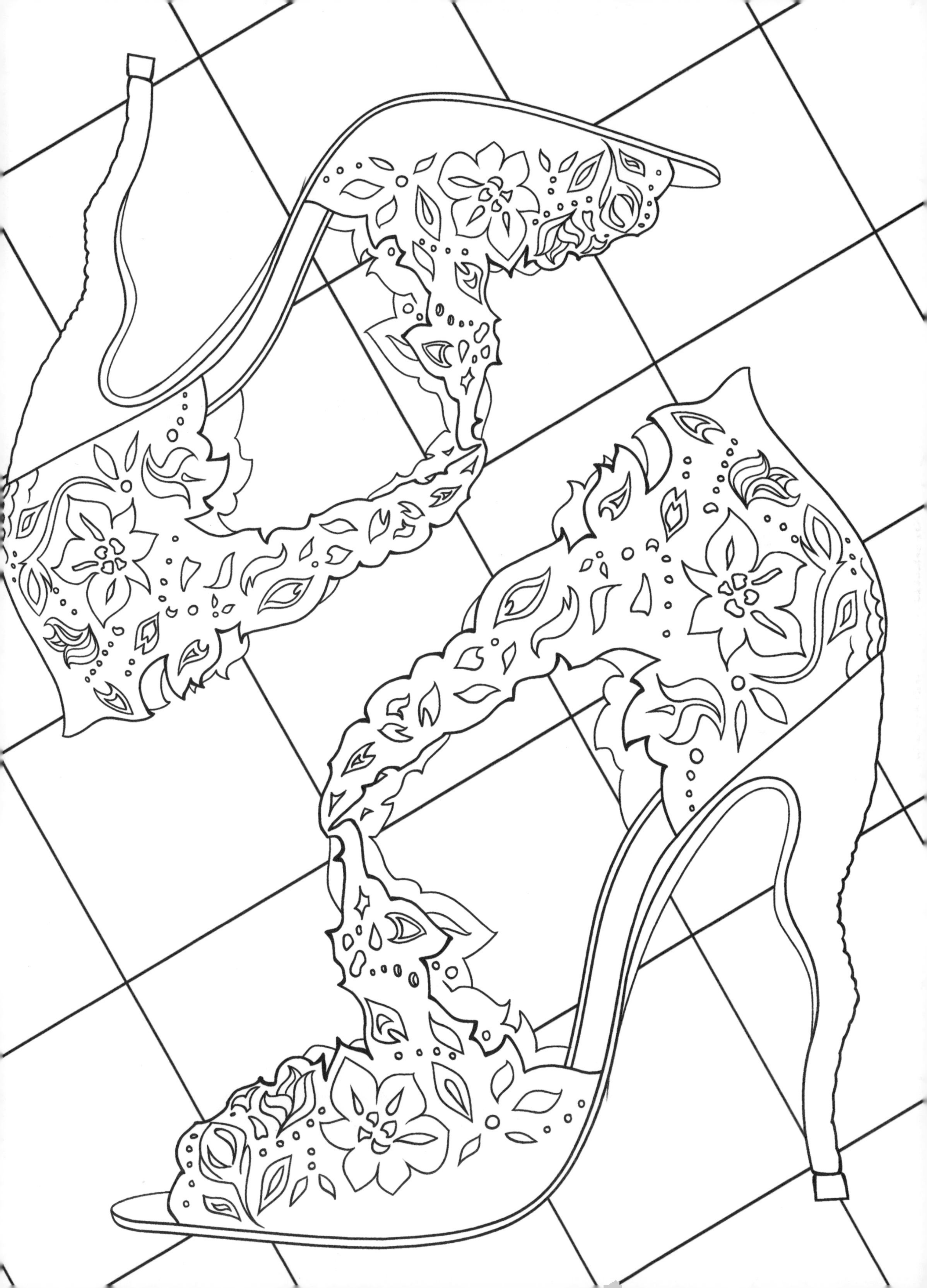

Garance

LOLITA

HUILE
ABSOLUE

1er. ARRt

RUE ÉTIENNE MARCEL

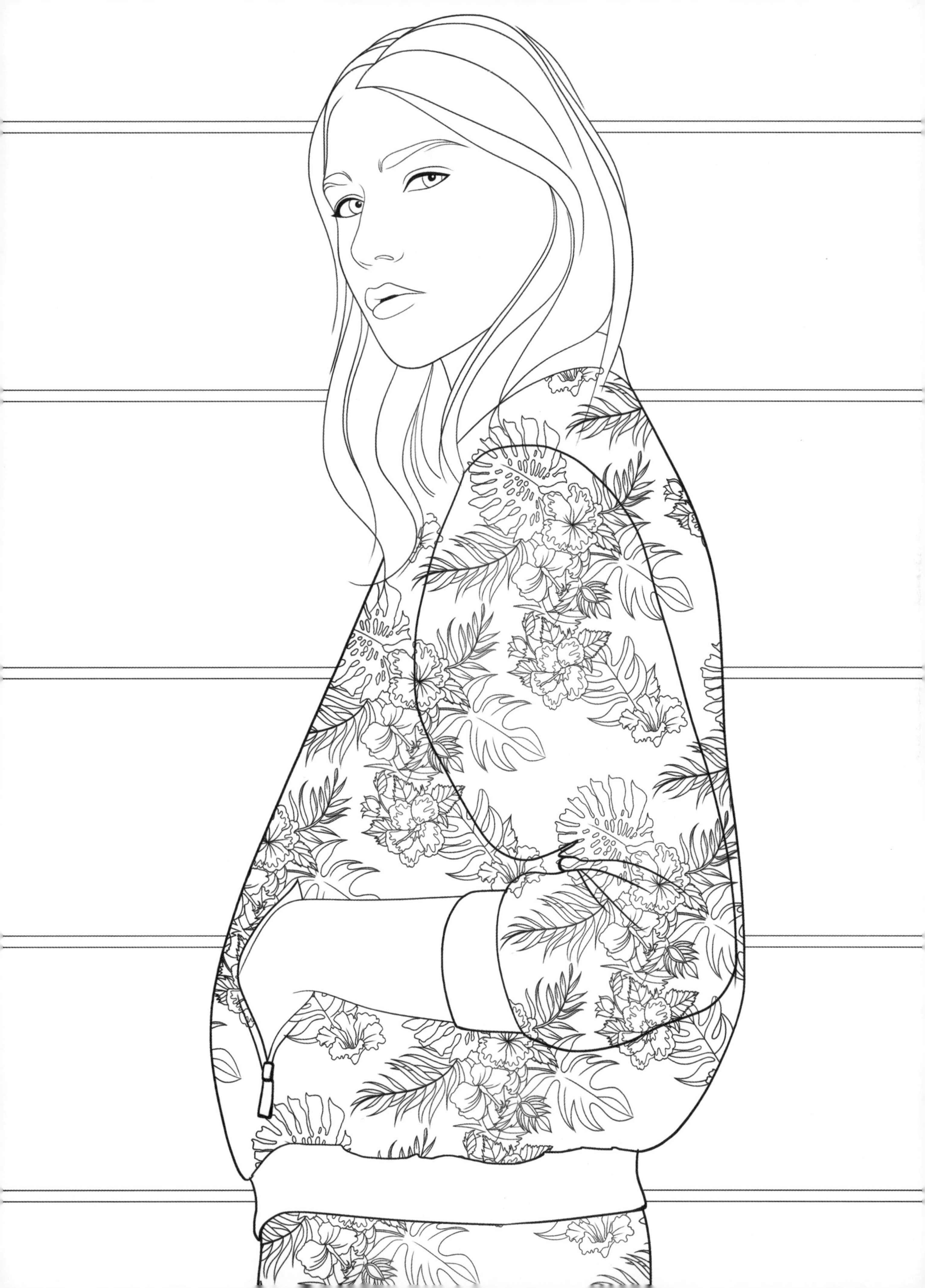

PICTURE YOURSELF ON THE COVER OF A MAGAZINE

PARIS
MAGAZINE

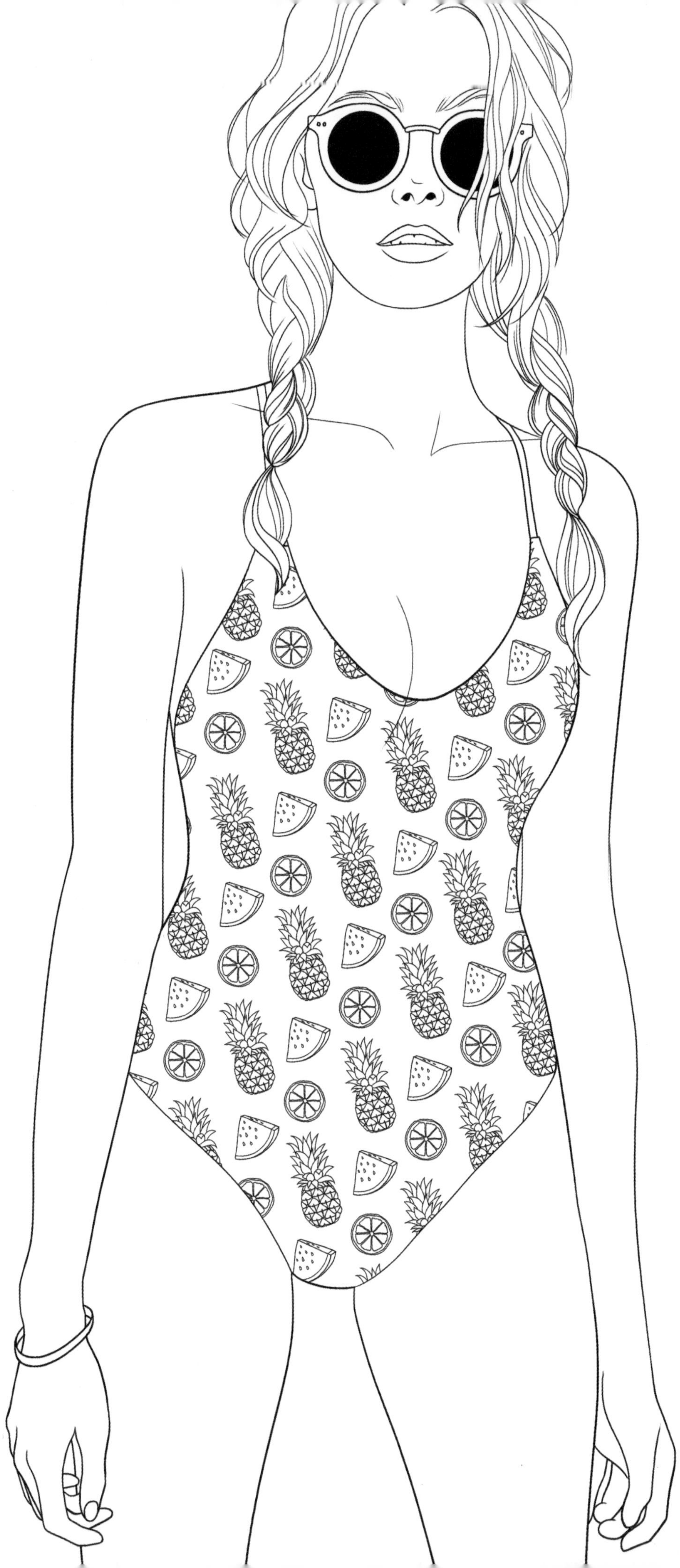

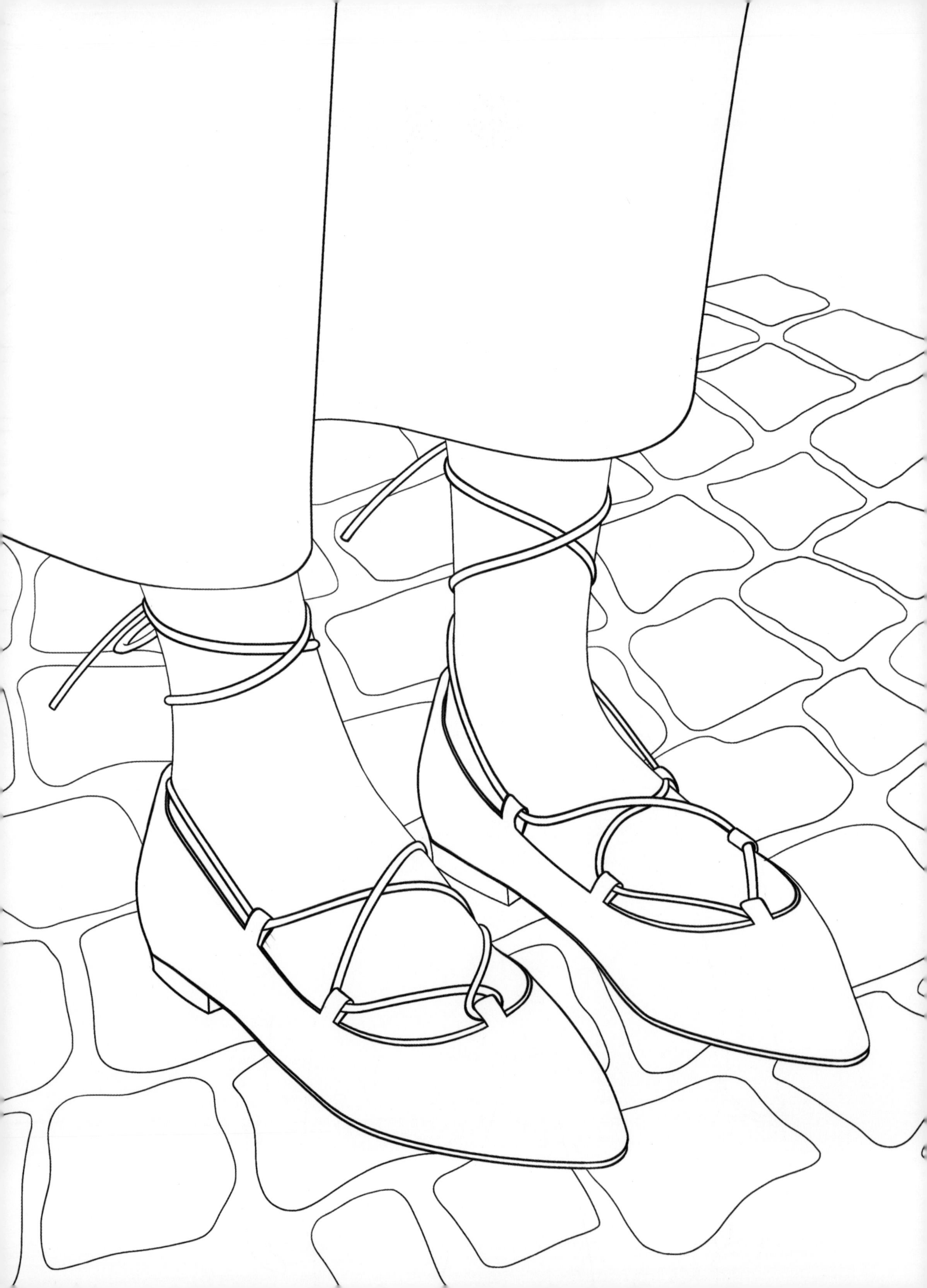

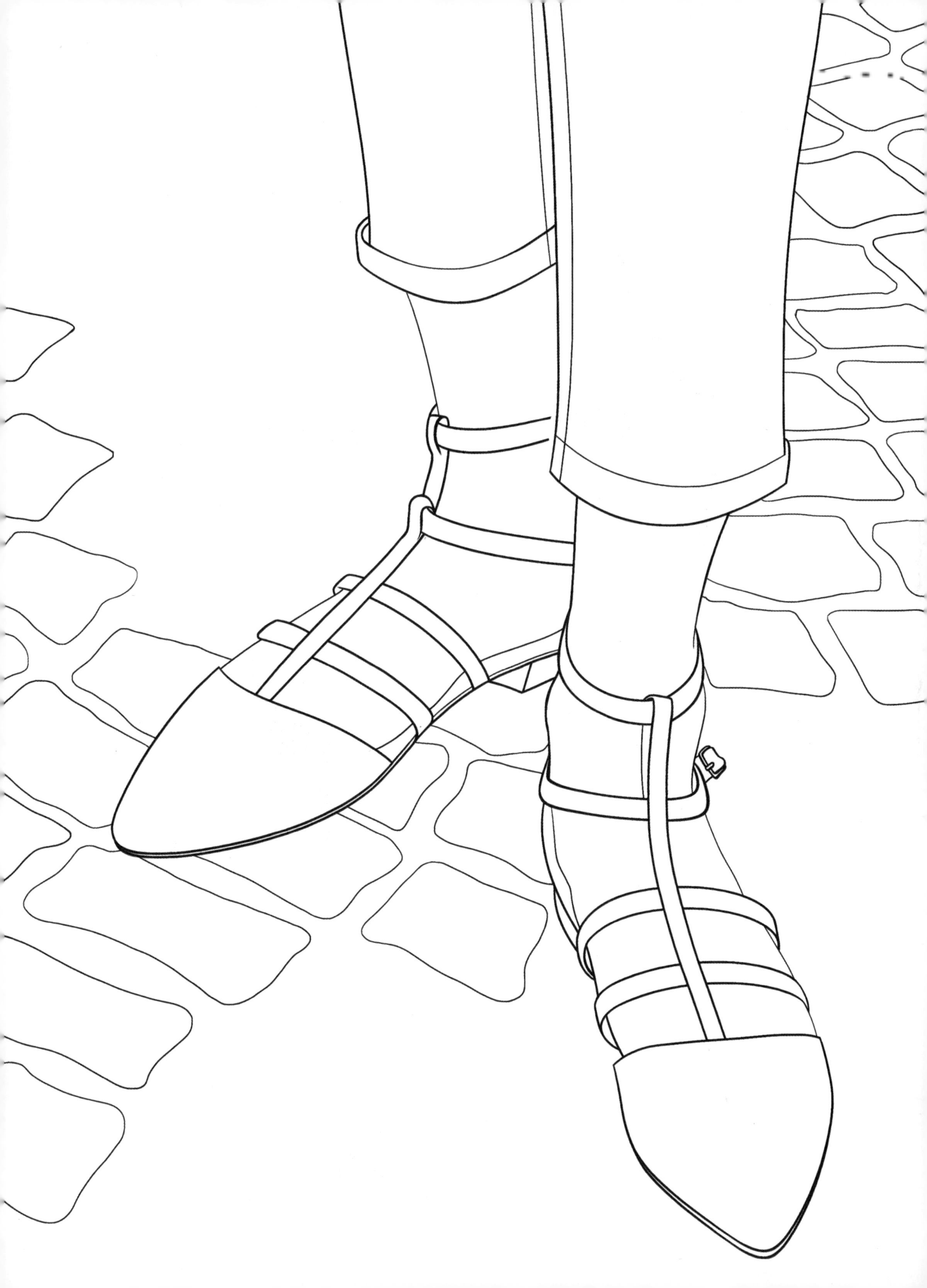

LÉA Seydoux

Mirbeau
Le Journal
d'une femme de chambre

classique

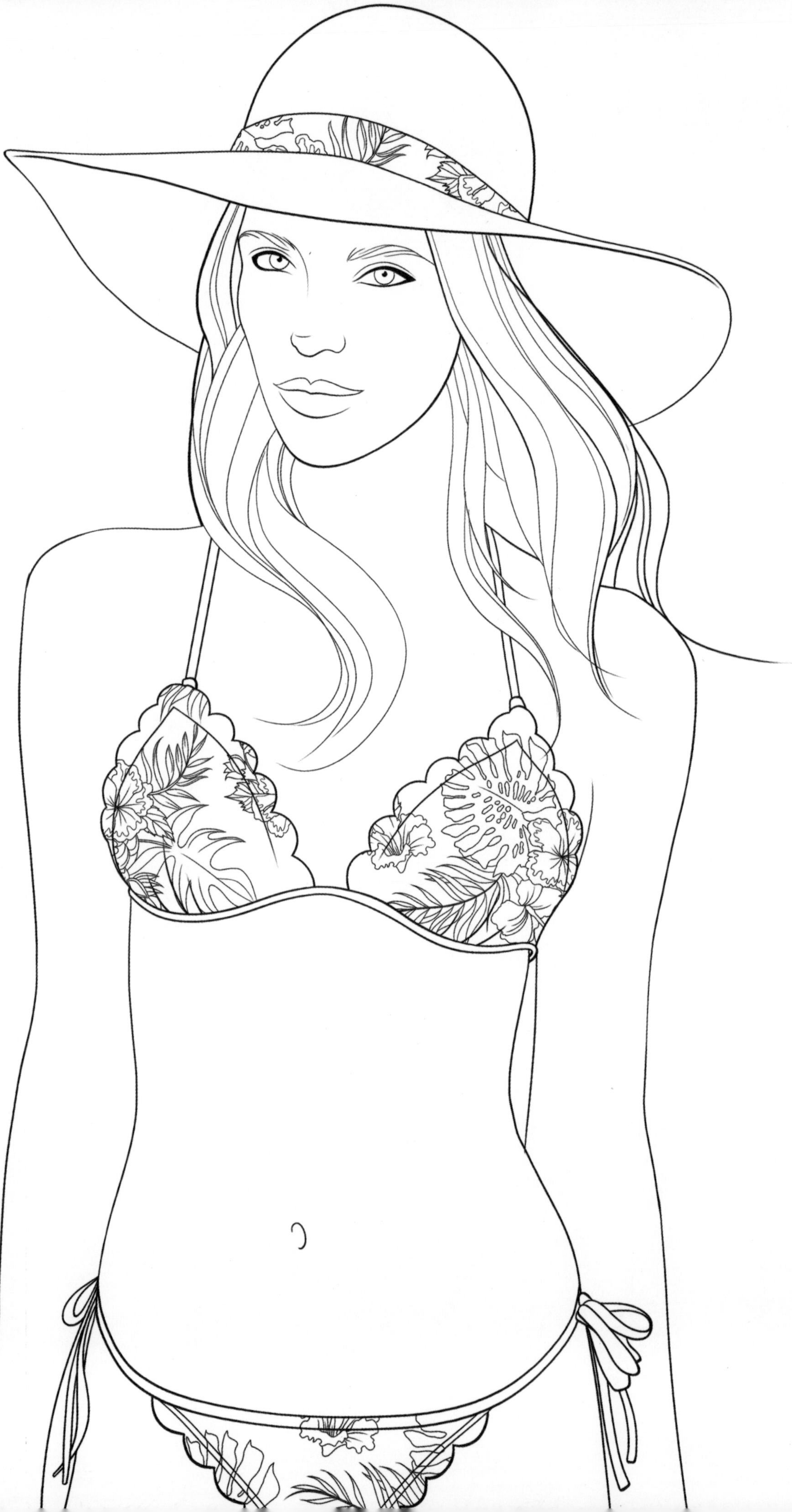

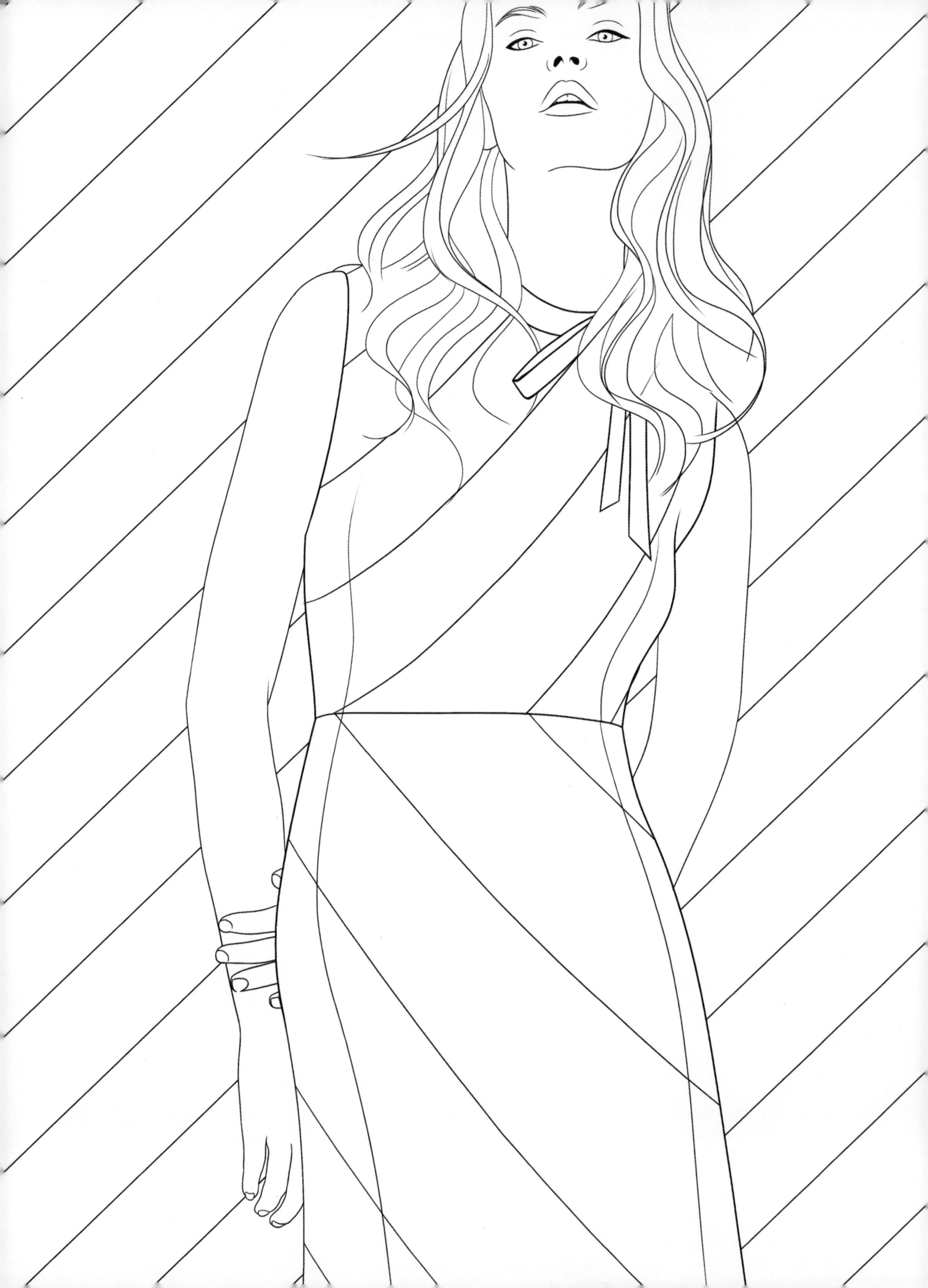

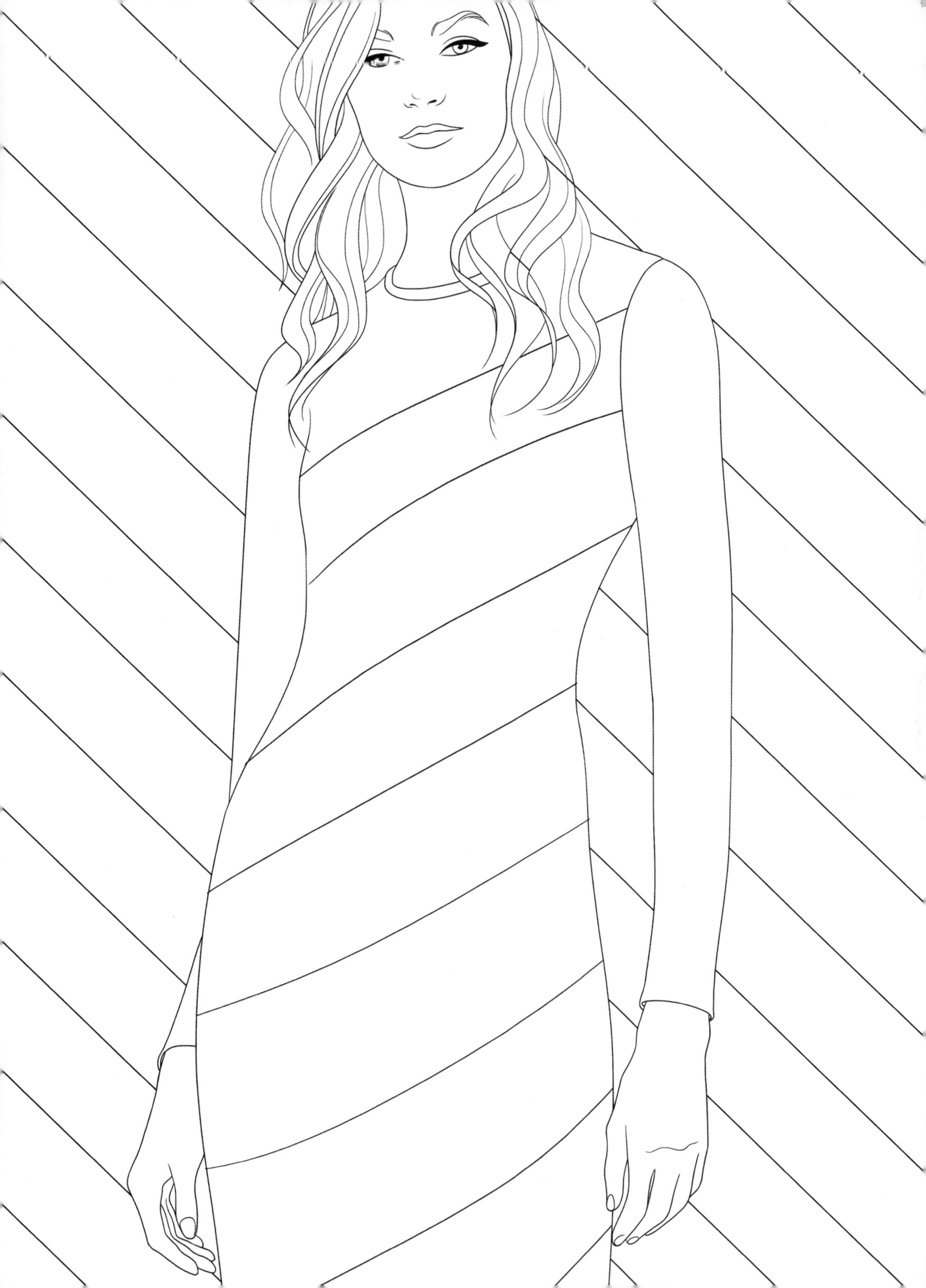

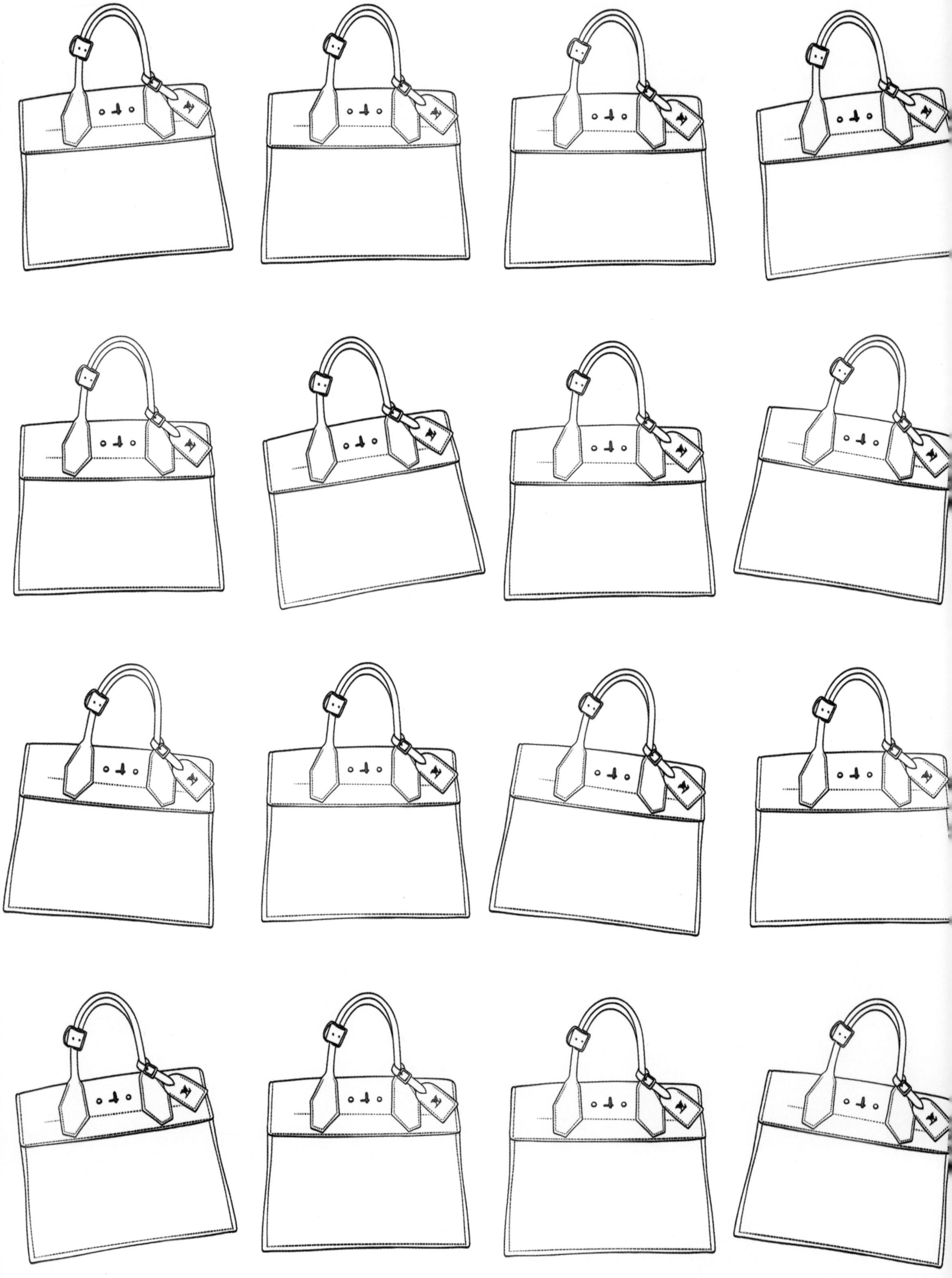

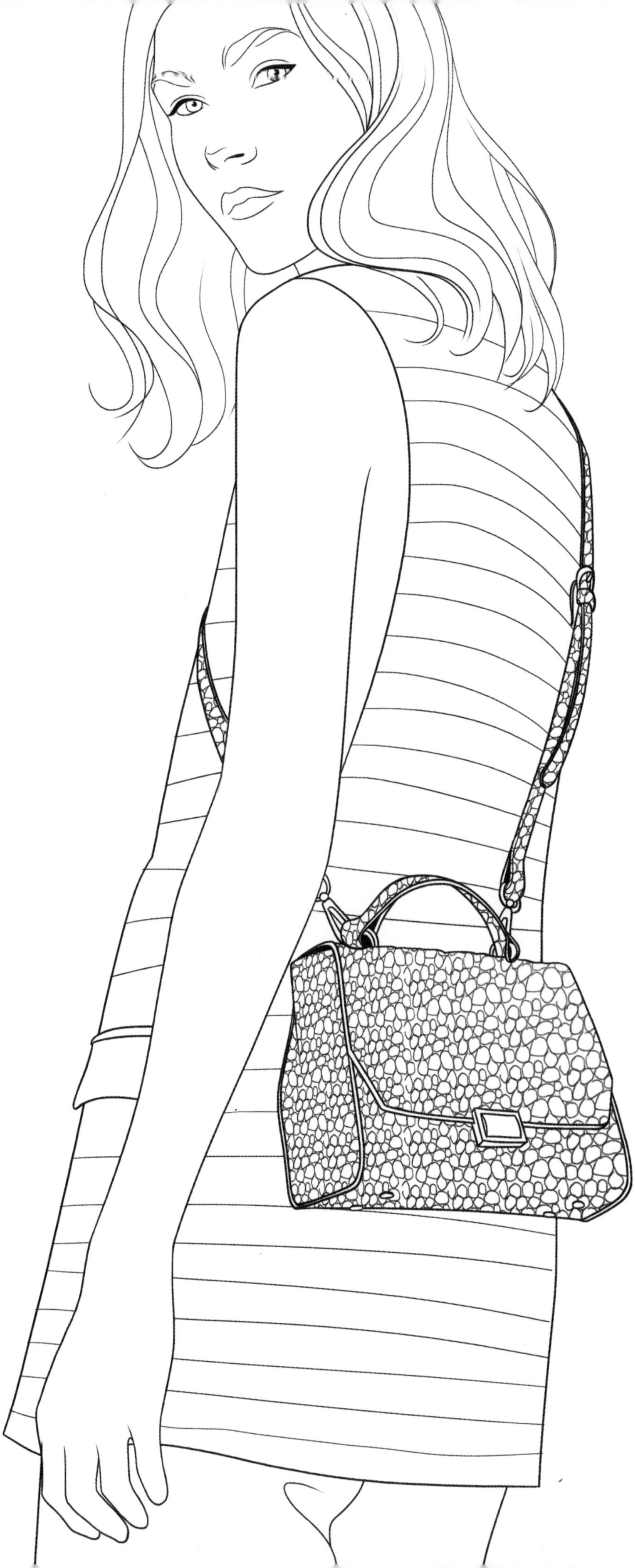

#CARNETDEMODEPARISIENNE

POST YOUR FINISHED CREATIONS ON SOCIAL MEDIA WITH THE HASHTAG

#CARNETDEMODEPARISIENNE

Merci à Isabelle Adjani, Jane Birkin, Catherine Deneuve, Charlotte Gainsbourg, Françoise Hardy, Léa Seydoux, Ariane Dubois, Marine Hannah Lottermoser, Garance Rochoux-Moreau, Chanel, Ladurée, Schott N-Y, Caroline Levesque, Anne Serroy, et Maxime...

Clément Dezelus

First English Edition Published by Gingko Press, September 2017
Gingko Press, Inc.
1321 Fifth Street
Berkeley, CA 94710, USA
www.gingkopress.com
ISBN: 978-1-58423-672-6
Printed in China

Originally Published as "Carnet de Mode Parisienne"
© 2016, Éditions de La Martinière, un marque de la société EDLM